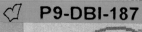

KATE GREENAWAY
Cross Stitch Designs
Julie Hasler

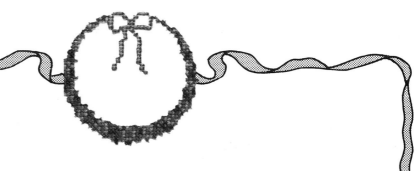

KATE GREENAWAY
Cross Stitch Designs

Julie Hasler

A DAVID & CHARLES CRAFT BOOK

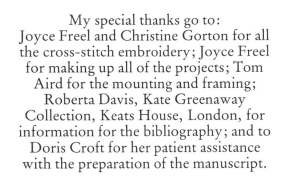

My special thanks go to:
Joyce Freel and Christine Gorton for all
the cross-stitch embroidery; Joyce Freel
for making up all of the projects; Tom
Aird for the mounting and framing;
Roberta Davis, Kate Greenaway
Collection, Keats House, London, for
information for the bibliography; and to
Doris Croft for her patient assistance
with the preparation of the manuscript.

British Library Cataloguing in Publication Data
Hasler, Julie S.
    Kate Greenaway cross-stitch designs. – (A David &
Charles craft book).
    1. Embroidery. Cross-stitch. Designs based on
illustrations for children's stories in English,
1837-1900. Patterns
I. Title
    746.44

ISBN 0–7153–9325–1

First published 1989
Second impression 1989
Third impression 1990

Photographs by Di Lewis

© Julie S. Hasler 1989

Typeset by ABM Typographics Ltd, Hull
and printed in West Germany
by Mohndruck GmbH
for David & Charles   Newton Abbot   Devon

Distributed in the United States by
Sterling Publishing Co Inc,
387 Park Avenue South, New York, NY 10016-8810

CONTENTS

KATE GREENAWAY
(1846–1901)

Born in London in 1846, Kate Greenaway was a brilliant artist and illustrator, exhibiting her work at the Royal Academy from 1877. She had a very special gift for finding beauty in the things around her and for conveying this rose-tinted view of life and nature to others. Her drawings of both children and flowers were sensitively observed and executed with a fresh and delicate use of colour so that her work was praised by art critics throughout the world.

By the 1880s, Kate Greenaway had become the darling of the Victorians and her popular books were being produced in editions of over ten thousand. Her idyllic vision of

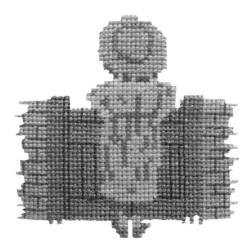

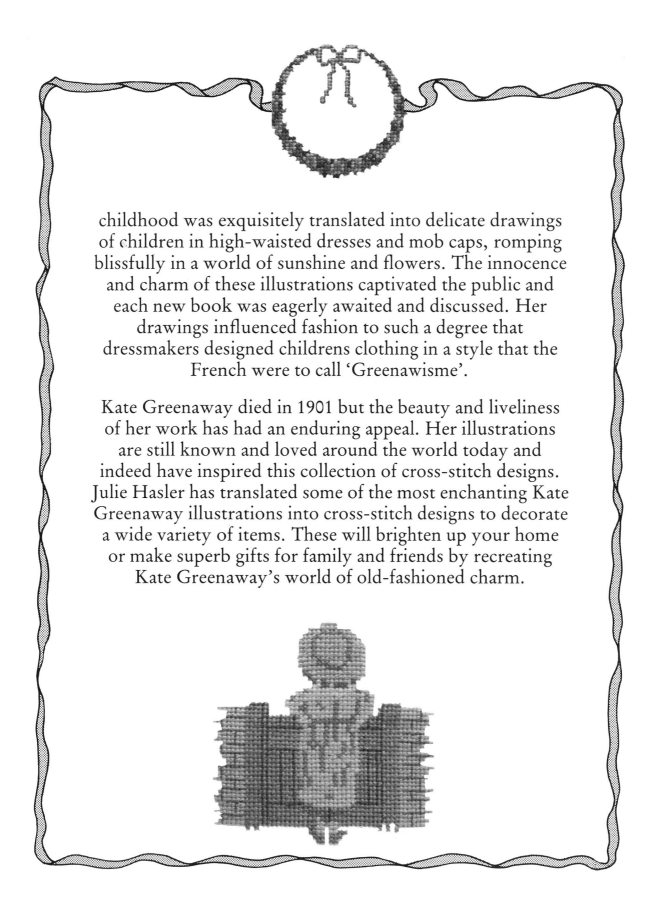

childhood was exquisitely translated into delicate drawings of children in high-waisted dresses and mob caps, romping blissfully in a world of sunshine and flowers. The innocence and charm of these illustrations captivated the public and each new book was eagerly awaited and discussed. Her drawings influenced fashion to such a degree that dressmakers designed childrens clothing in a style that the French were to call 'Greenawisme'.

Kate Greenaway died in 1901 but the beauty and liveliness of her work has had an enduring appeal. Her illustrations are still known and loved around the world today and indeed have inspired this collection of cross-stitch designs. Julie Hasler has translated some of the most enchanting Kate Greenaway illustrations into cross-stitch designs to decorate a wide variety of items. These will brighten up your home or make superb gifts for family and friends by recreating Kate Greenaway's world of old-fashioned charm.

INTRODUCTION

Cross-stitch is a very simple, versatile and elegant needlecraft – a rewarding and inexpensive hobby. Both experienced and inexperienced needleworkers will find projects in this book to suit their abilities. If you are a complete novice and have never attempted cross-stitch before, take care to read the next few sections thoroughly before you begin. Take your time. If you have difficulty in absorbing all the information at first, refer back to the relevant section to check the details. The section entitled 'Important Advice' on p14 will prove very helpful.

The designs illustrated in this book show many refreshing ways in which cross-stitch can be used to decorate the home, or to make children's clothes or unusual gifts. Included in the many projects are a set of four lace-trimmed cushions, a child's cot quilt, lavender bags, pictures, trinket boxes and a child's skirt. All the items are beautifully

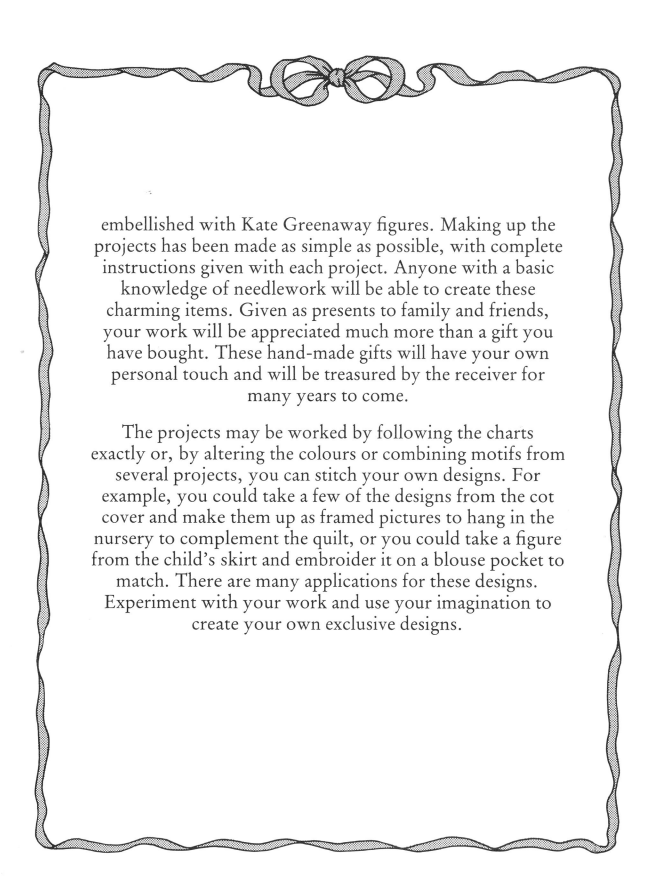

embellished with Kate Greenaway figures. Making up the projects has been made as simple as possible, with complete instructions given with each project. Anyone with a basic knowledge of needlework will be able to create these charming items. Given as presents to family and friends, your work will be appreciated much more than a gift you have bought. These hand-made gifts will have your own personal touch and will be treasured by the receiver for many years to come.

The projects may be worked by following the charts exactly or, by altering the colours or combining motifs from several projects, you can stitch your own designs. For example, you could take a few of the designs from the cot cover and make them up as framed pictures to hang in the nursery to complement the quilt, or you could take a figure from the child's skirt and embroider it on a blouse pocket to match. There are many applications for these designs. Experiment with your work and use your imagination to create your own exclusive designs.

GENERAL DIRECTIONS

The charted designs in this book were originally created for counted cross-stitch, but they can easily be translated into other needlework techniques such as needlepoint, crochet and knitting, to name but a few.

In the counted-thread work, the finished piece of work will not be the same size as the charted design unless you are working with canvas or fabric which has the same amount of threads per inch as the chart has squares per inch.

The size of the finished piece of work will vary with crochet and knitting according to the number of stitches per inch.

MATERIALS

NEEDLES
A small blunt tapestry needle, No 24 or No 26.

FABRIC
Even-weave fabrics are used for cross-stitch such as Aida, Hardanger and Ainring. The type of fabric to be used is given with each project.

THREADS
The charted designs in this book have been keyed to shades of DMC stranded cotton, which is six stranded. The amount of strands used in the work will depend on the fabric used. Details of this are given with each project.

EMBROIDERY HOOP
For cross-stitch, it is best to use a 10, 13 or 15cm (4in, 5in or 6in) round wooden or plastic hoop with a screw-type tension adjuster.

SCISSORS
A pair of sharp embroidery scissors is essential, especially if a mistake has to be cut out.

PREPARING TO WORK

The following steps will allow you to achieve a much better coverage of your fabric.

To prevent the fabric from ravelling, the edges can either be covered with a fold of masking tape, or whip-stitched or machine-stitched. It is important where you make the first stitch, as it will place the finished design on your fabric. Find the exact centre point of the chart by following the arrows to their intersection . Locate the centre of the fabric by folding it in half vertically and then horizontally, pinching along the folds. The centre stitch of the chart will be where the creases in the fabric meet. Mark along these lines with basting stitches if necessary (see p15).

It is preferable to begin cross-stitch at the top of the design. To locate the top, count the squares up from the centre of the chart, then count left or right to the first symbol. Count the corresponding number of holes up and across from the centre of the

fabric and begin at that point. Remember that each square on the chart represents a stitch to be made on the fabric.

Place the fabric in the embroidery hoop, gently pull it taut and tighten the screw. You will find it easier to have the screw in the '10-o-clock' position to prevent the thread from becoming tangled in the screw with each stitch. However, if you are left-handed, have the screw in the '1-o-clock' position. While working, you will find it necessary to continue retightening the fabric to keep it taut, as tension makes it easier to push the needle through the holes without piercing the fibres.

When working with stranded cotton, always separate the strands and place them together again before threading your needle and beginning to stitch. Always use separate strands, never double thread. For example, if you need to use two strands, use two separate strands, not one doubled up.

METHOD

To make the stitch, bring the needle up from the wrong side, through a hole in the fabric (see Fig 1) at the left end of a row of stitches of the same colour. Fasten the thread by holding a short length of thread on the underside of the fabric and secure it with the first two or three stitches as

in Fig 2. Never knot your thread as this will create a bumpy back surface and prevent your work from lying flat when it is finished. Next bring the needle across one block (or square) to the right and one block above on a left to right diagonal as in Fig 1. Half the stitch is now

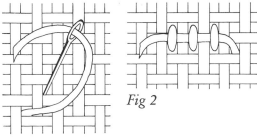

Fig 2

Fig 1

rows of stitches are worked as shown in Fig 5.

Fig 5

completed. Continue in this way until you reach the end of the row. Your stitches will be diagonal on the right side of the fabric and vertical stitches on the wrong side. Complete the stitch by crossing back from right to left to form an X as in Fig 3. Work all the stitches in the row by completing the Xs as in Fig 4.

Backstitch is used for outlines, face and hand details etc. It is worked from hole to hole and can be stitched in horizontal, vertical or diagonal lines as shown in Fig 6.

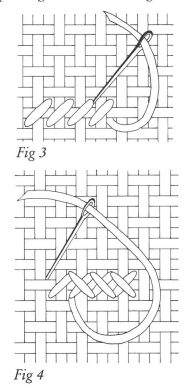

Fig 3

Fig 4

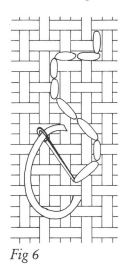

Fig 6

Cross-stitch can also be worked by crossing each stitch as you come to it, as you would do for isolated stitches. This method works just as well – it is really a personal preference. Vertical

Finish all threads by running your needle under four or more stitches on the reverse side of your work as in Fig 7 and cut close.

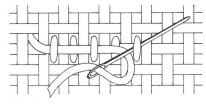

Fig 7

IMPORTANT ADVICE

1 When stitching, be careful not to pull the fabric out of shape. Work the stitches in two motions, straight up through a hole in the fabric and then straight down ensuring that the fabric remains taut. Do not pull the thread taut – it should be snug, but not tight. Using this method, the thread will lie just where you want it to and will not pull your fabric out of shape.

2 If the thread becomes twisted during working, drop the needle and let it hang down so that it untwists by itself. Twisted thread will appear thinner and will not cover the fabric as well.

3 Do not leave the needle in the design area of your work when it is not in use. No matter how good the needle might be, it may rust in time.

4 When carrying thread from one area to another, finish off and begin again. Do not carry thread across an open expanse of fabric. Loose threads, especially dark colours, will be visible from the front of your work when the project is completed.

5 Backstitch is worked when the cross-stitch embroidery has been completed. Always use one strand less than that used in the embroidery. For example, if you have used three strands of stranded cotton to work the cross-stitch embroidery, use two strands for the backstitching. If one strand of stranded cotton is used to work the cross-stitch embroidery, one strand is also used for the backstitching. Always take care not to pull the backstitches too tight, otherwise the contrast of colour will be lost against the cross-stitches.

6 When you have completed the cross-stitch embroideries, you may need to press them. To protect the embroideries when you press them, place them right side down onto a soft towel and cover the reverse side with a slightly damp cloth.

STITCHES USED

RUNNING STITCH

Running stitch is short and closely spaced, giving the illusion of an unbroken line. Use a thread that matches your fabric. To avoid tangling, use a single thread no more than 50cm (19½in) long. The stitches should be fine, approximately 2mm (⅛in) long and evenly spaced on both the top and reverse sides. When you become familiar with this stitch, your working speed can be increased by picking up several stitches on the needle before pushing it through.

Running stitch

BASTING/TACKING STITCH

Basting or tacking stitches are also sewn by hand. They are used temporarily to hold layers of fabric, lace, wadding, etc, in a particular position. The stitches are removed once the project is complete. Use a contrasting colour of thread that is easy to see.

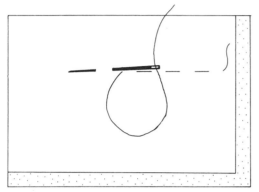

Basting/tacking

WHIP STITCH

Whip stitch over the edge of your fabric using double strands of thread to match the fabric. The stitches should be evenly spaced, no more than 6mm (¼in) apart. Fasten the end of the thread with a knot.

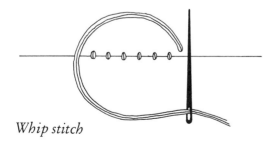

Whip stitch

OVERSEWING

Working from right to left, bring the needle out of the fabric just above the edge. Insert the needle below, making a horizontal stitch to the left. Place the needle back into the hole it came out of and make a diagonal stitch up and to the left.

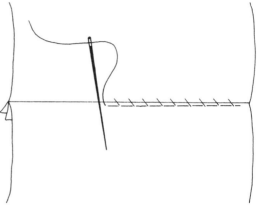

Oversewing

SLIP STITCH

Slip stitching is used to join two pieces of fabric together by hand and gives an almost invisible finish. Insert the needle at A, slide 4-7mm (⅛-¼in) through the folded edge of the fabric and bring out at B. Directly below B, make a small stitch through the second piece of fabric.

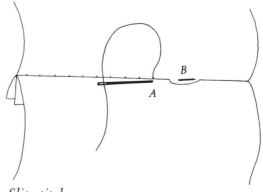

Slip stitch

LACE TRIMMED CUSHIONS

These beautiful lace and satin cushions are simple to make and will brighten up any room. Each one has a slightly different border and its own central design: Lamb, Duck, Two Maids and Young Lady with Dog. They make a charming set.
(Charts 1–4)

MATERIALS

For each cushion you will require:
1m (39in) cream satin
1.20m (47½in) frilled lace 76mm (3in) wide
1 cushion 38 x 38cm (15 x 15in)
1 19cm (7½in) square of cream Ainring with 18 stitches to the inch
DMC 6-strand stranded cotton
Sewing thread to match the fabric

All measurements include a 1cm (½in) seam allowance.

DIRECTIONS

1 Complete the cross-stitch embroidery using two strands of the stranded cotton.

2 From the cream satin, cut pieces as follows:
Back: 1 piece 40 x 40cm
  (15¾ x 15¾in)
Sides: 2 pieces 12.5 x 19cm
  (5 x 7¾in)
Top and bottom: 2 pieces 12.5 x 40cm
  (5 x 15¾in)

3 Sew each side piece to the central embroidered square and press the seams to the sides. The diagram shows the finished sizes of all pieces, after seam allowances have been taken.

4 Sew the top and bottom pieces in place and press the seams outwards.

5 Cut the lace into four strips each measuring 30cm (11¾in). Join these strips together, starting to stitch 5cm (2in) from the cut edge and slanting to a point at the outer edge of the lace as shown in Fig 1. Trim off any excess lace.

6 Place the lace square onto the

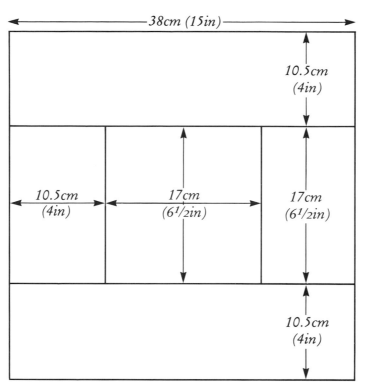

$\leftarrow$ 38cm (15in) $\rightarrow$

10.5cm (4in)

10.5cm (4in)   17cm (6¹/₂in)   17cm (6¹/₂in)

10.5cm (4in)

FINISHED CUSHION-COVER MEASUREMENTS
(after seam allowances taken)

cushion front 12mm (¹/₂in) from the stitched edge of the embroidered panel as shown in Fig 2. Tack and machine stitch into place. Remove the tacking stitches.

7 With wrong sides together, join the three sides of the front and back cushion-cover pieces, being careful not to catch in the edges of the lace. Turn to the right side and press.

8 Catch stitch the corners of the lace on the corners of the cushion-cover.

9 Press in the seam allowance on the open edge, place the cushion inside the cover and hand oversew the open edge closed.

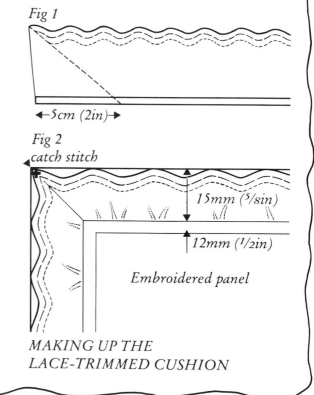

Fig 1

$\leftarrow$ 5cm (2in) $\rightarrow$

Fig 2

catch stitch

15mm (⁵/₈in)

12mm (¹/₂in)

Embroidered panel

MAKING UP THE
LACE-TRIMMED CUSHION

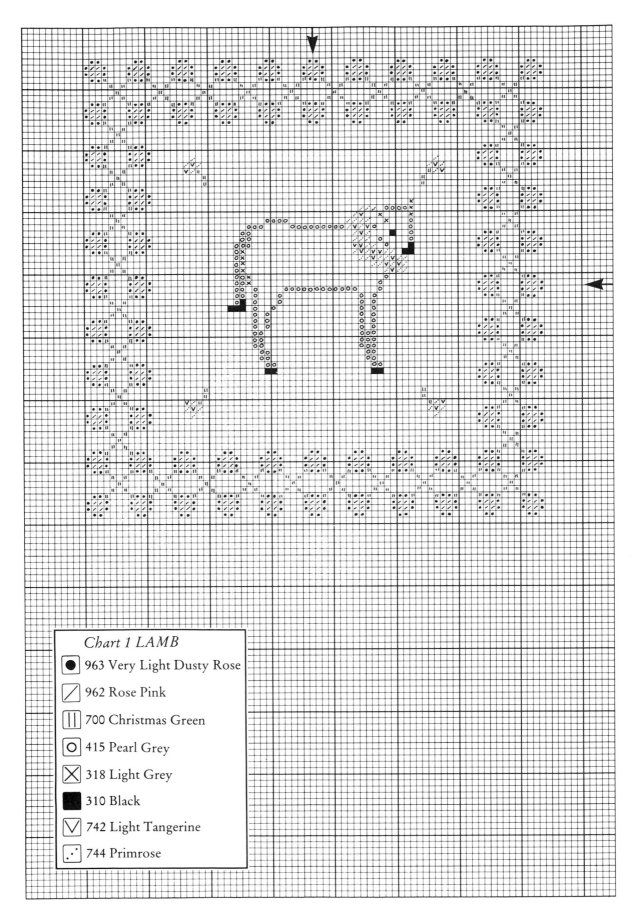

Chart 1 LAMB

- ● 963 Very Light Dusty Rose
- ╱ 962 Rose Pink
- ‖ 700 Christmas Green
- ◯ 415 Pearl Grey
- ☒ 318 Light Grey
- ■ 310 Black
- ⋁ 742 Light Tangerine
- ⋰ 744 Primrose

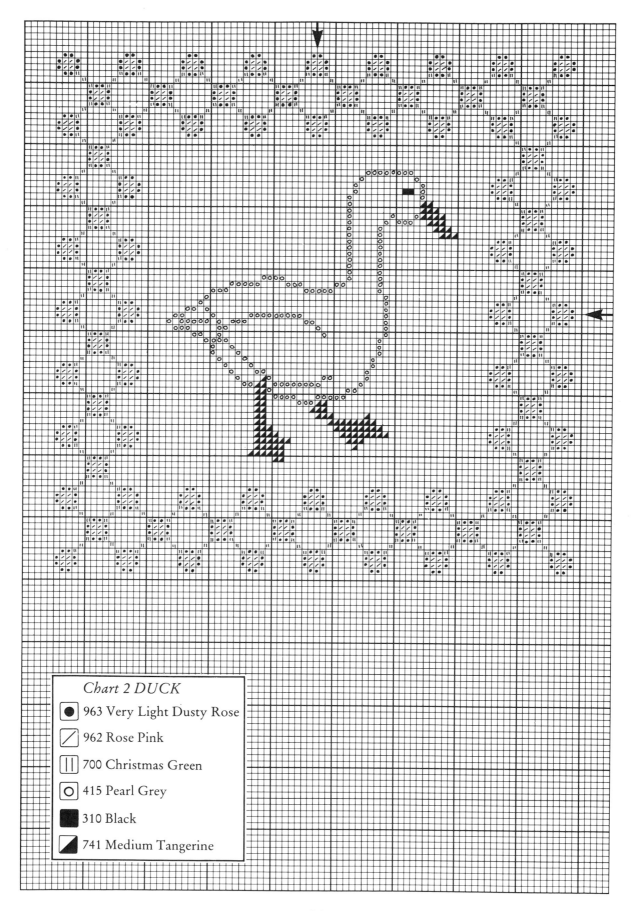

Chart 2 DUCK

- ● 963 Very Light Dusty Rose
- ╱ 962 Rose Pink
- ‖ 700 Christmas Green
- ○ 415 Pearl Grey
- ■ 310 Black
- ◢ 741 Medium Tangerine

LAMB

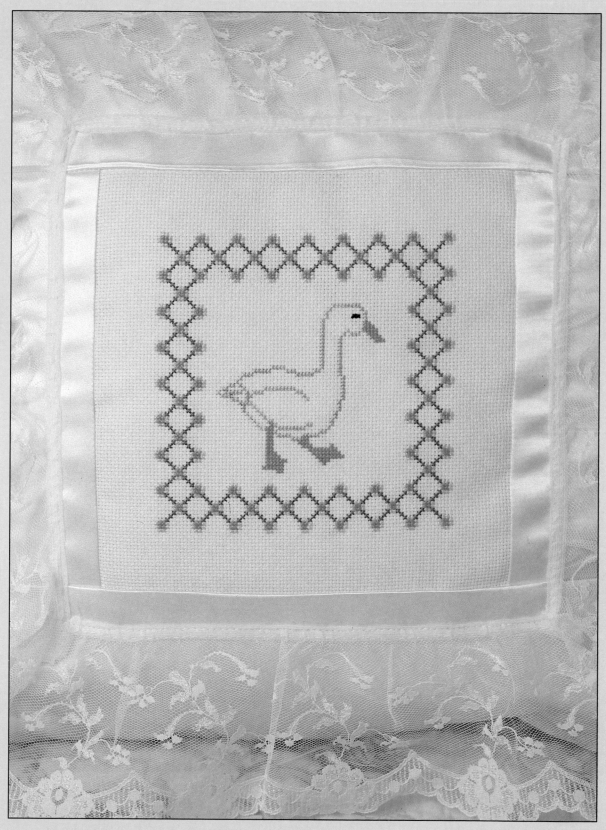

DUCK

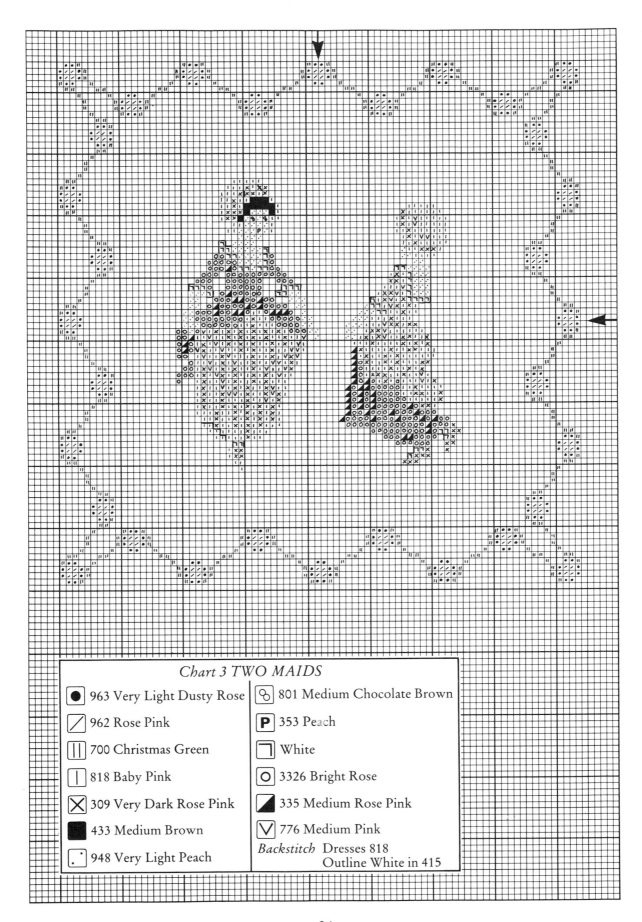

Chart 3 TWO MAIDS

●	963 Very Light Dusty Rose	🕈	801 Medium Chocolate Brown
╱	962 Rose Pink	P	353 Peach
‖	700 Christmas Green	⌐	White
│	818 Baby Pink	O	3326 Bright Rose
✕	309 Very Dark Rose Pink	◢	335 Medium Rose Pink
■	433 Medium Brown	V	776 Medium Pink
⠌	948 Very Light Peach		*Backstitch* Dresses 818
			Outline White in 415

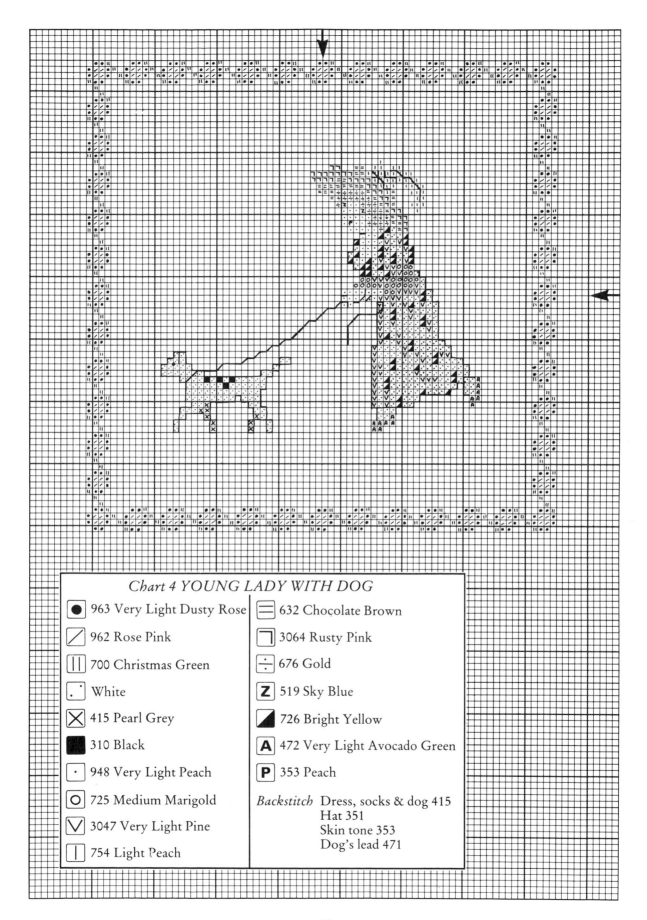

Chart 4 YOUNG LADY WITH DOG

●	963 Very Light Dusty Rose	⊟	632 Chocolate Brown
╱	962 Rose Pink	⊓	3064 Rusty Pink
‖	700 Christmas Green	÷	676 Gold
·	White	Z	519 Sky Blue
✕	415 Pearl Grey	◣	726 Bright Yellow
■	310 Black	A	472 Very Light Avocado Green
·	948 Very Light Peach	P	353 Peach
O	725 Medium Marigold		
V	3047 Very Light Pine		
│	754 Light Peach		

Backstitch Dress, socks & dog 415
Hat 351
Skin tone 353
Dog's lead 471

TWO MAIDS

YOUNG LADY WITH DOG

COT QUILT

An embroidered quilt is a delightful addition to any child's room. The following directions are for making up the quilt exactly as shown in the photograph. You can alter the quilt to your own personal taste by altering the order of the embroideries on the quilt or by selecting three or four designs and arranging them to your choice. You can also change the colour of the borders and backing. For example, instead of using pink for a girl's room, as shown, you could use blue for a boy's room or a contrasting patterned or floral print. Whatever your choice, this beautiful quilt will give great pleasure for many years. (Charts 5–16)

MATERIALS
12 25 x 25cm (10 x 10in) squares of white fine Aida with 14 stitches to the inch. These measurements include 12mm (½in) seam allowance. When made up the square will measure 23 x 23cm (9 x 9in)
2m (78¾in) of 152cm (60in) wide fabric for backing and dividers
1.3m (51¼in) of wadding 1m (39½in) wide
DMC 6-strand stranded cotton
Sewing cotton to match the fabric

DIRECTIONS
Complete all your cross-stitch embroideries using two strands of stranded cotton and carefully press them.
Position the designs 1–12 as shown in the photograph of the finished quilt. For the backing and dividers, cut the fabric as follows (see Fig 1).

   A: 8 pieces 9 x 25cm (3½ x 9¾in)
   B: 3 pieces 9 x 85cm (3½ x 33½in)
   C: 2 pieces 10cm x 1.15m
       (4 x 45¼in)
   D: 2 pieces 10cm x 1.01m
       (4 x 39¾in)

   E: 1 piece 1.01 x 1.31m
       (39¾ x 51½in)
These measurements include a seam allowance on all edges.
Assemble the quilt front as shown in Fig 2.

1 Sew the embroidered blocks and the vertical dividers (A) together to form horizontal strips.

2 Sew the horizontal strips and the horizontal dividers (B) together.

3 Add the sides (C).

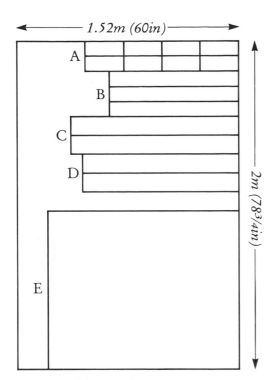

Fig 1 COT QUILT:
FABRIC CUTTING GUIDE

1.52m (60in)

A

B

C

D

E

2m (78¾in)

4 Finally add the top and bottom borders (D).

5 Press all the seams towards the squares.

Assembling the quilt
Lay the backing piece of fabric (E) right side down on a flat surface, placing the wadding on top.
Place the completed quilt front on top of the wadding right side up.
Ensure that all edges are even.
Pin and tack all the fabrics together around the squares.
Quilt around each square by hand, using small running stitches to penetrate all the layers. Remove the pins and tacking stitches.

FINISHING

Fold in a 6mm (¼in) seam allowance on all the edges of the quilt front over the wadding. Tack in place. It may be necessary to trim the wadding slightly to avoid too much bulk at the edges.
Fold in a 6mm (¼in) on all edges on the quilt backing.
Secure to front by tacking. Slip stitch all round, making sure that the stitches do not go through to the right side.

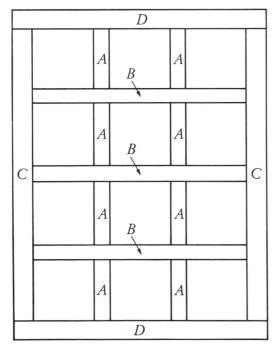

Fig 2 MAKING UP THE COT QUILT

915138

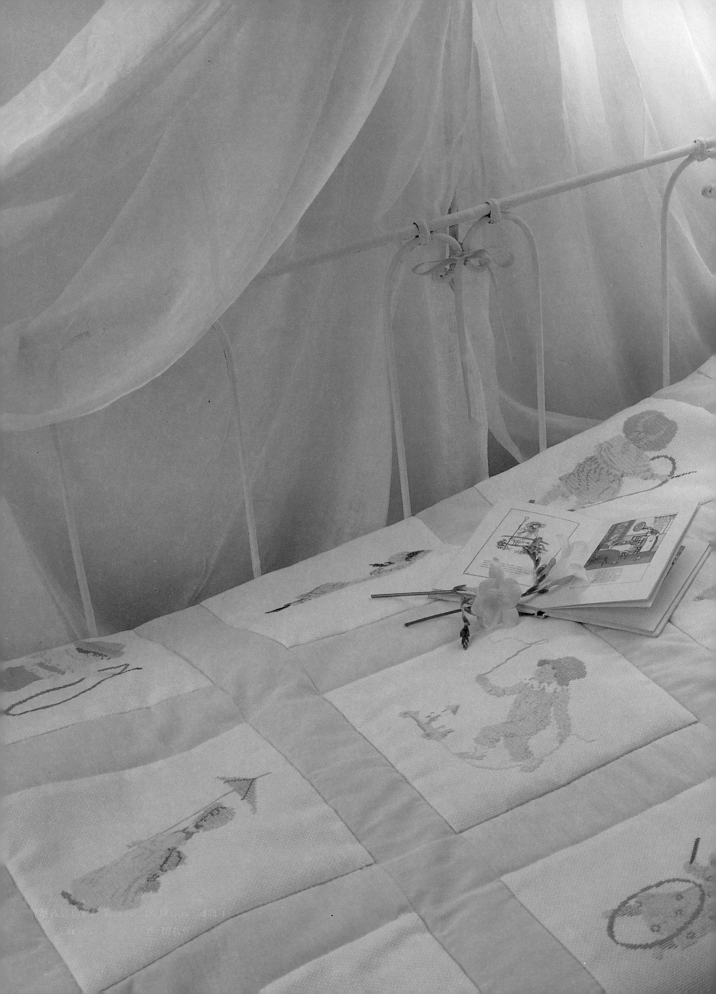

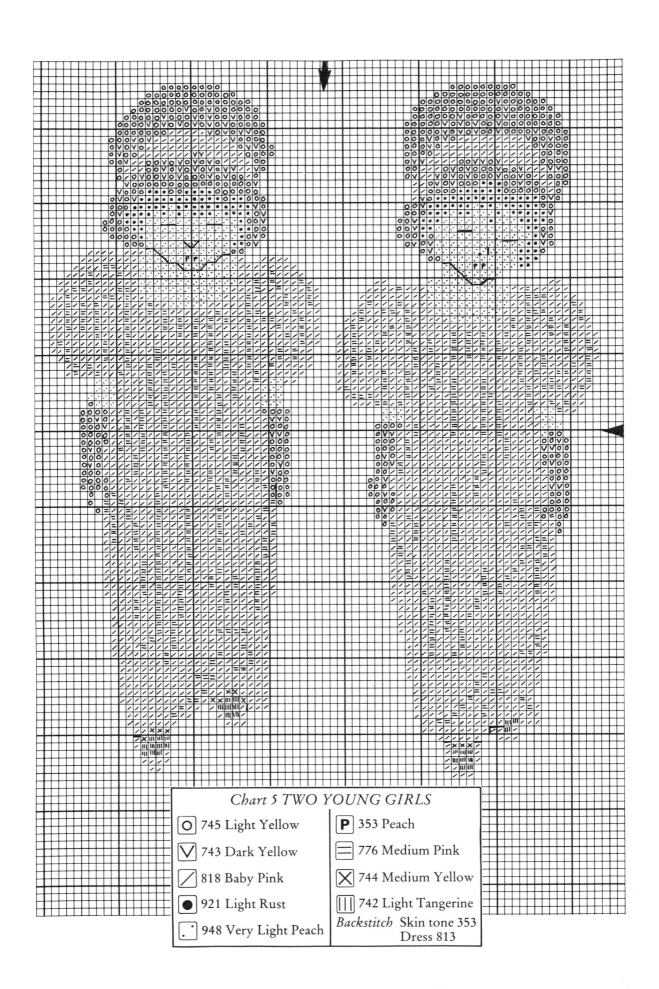

Chart 5 TWO YOUNG GIRLS

O	745 Light Yellow	P	353 Peach
V	743 Dark Yellow	=	776 Medium Pink
/	818 Baby Pink	X	744 Medium Yellow
●	921 Light Rust	|||	742 Light Tangerine
:	948 Very Light Peach	*Backstitch*	Skin tone 353
			Dress 813

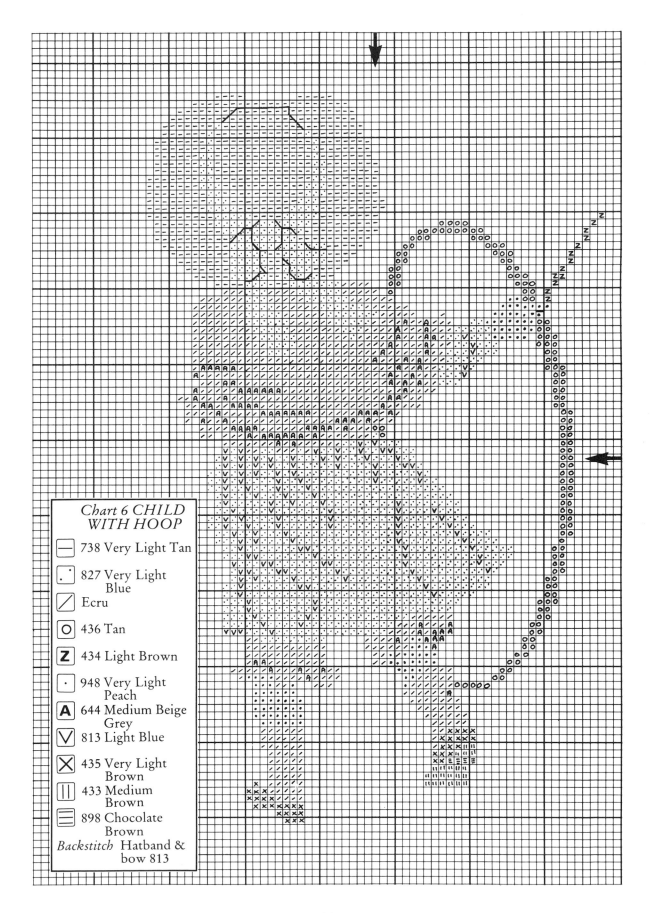

Chart 6 CHILD
WITH HOOP

—	738 Very Light Tan
·	827 Very Light Blue
╱	Ecru
O	436 Tan
Z	434 Light Brown
•	948 Very Light Peach
A	644 Medium Beige Grey
V	813 Light Blue
X	435 Very Light Brown
‖	433 Medium Brown
≡	898 Chocolate Brown

Backstitch Hatband & bow 813

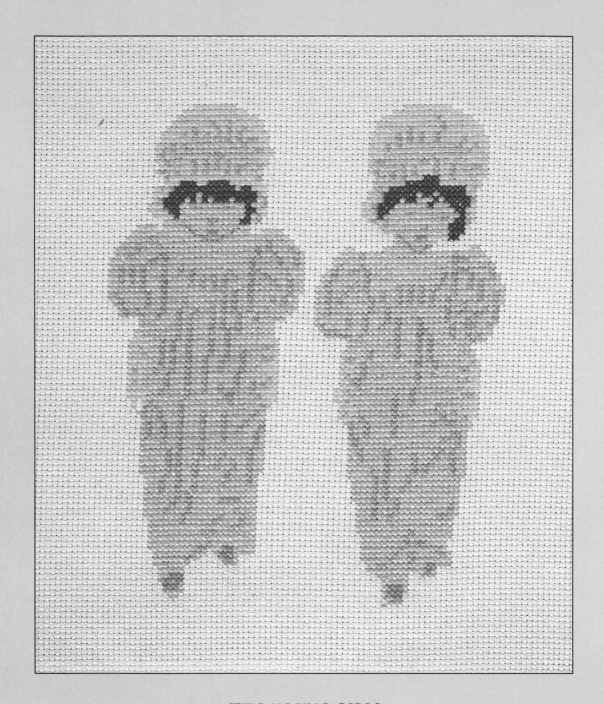

TWO YOUNG GIRLS

CHILD WITH HOOP

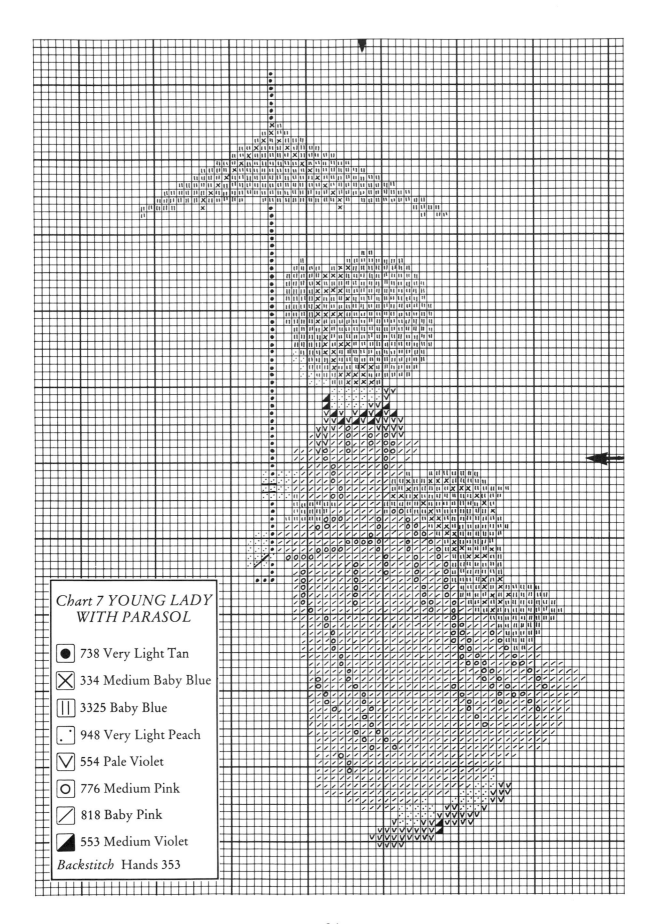

Chart 7 YOUNG LADY
WITH PARASOL

- ● 738 Very Light Tan
- ☒ 334 Medium Baby Blue
- ‖ 3325 Baby Blue
- ⚬ 948 Very Light Peach
- ∨ 554 Pale Violet
- ○ 776 Medium Pink
- ╱ 818 Baby Pink
- ◣ 553 Medium Violet

Backstitch Hands 353

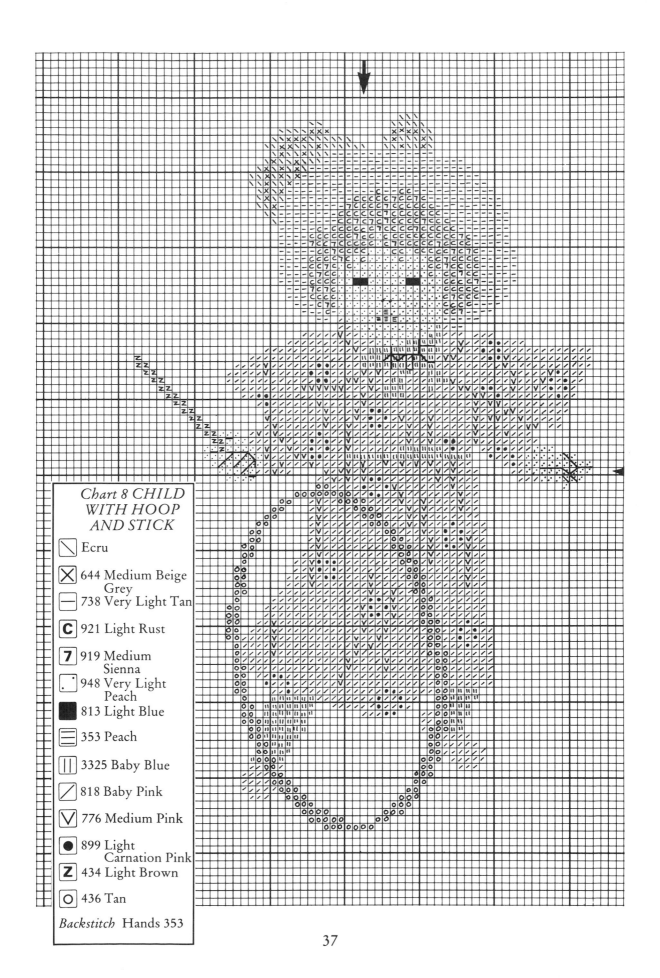

Chart 8 CHILD
WITH HOOP
AND STICK

⟍ Ecru

✕ 644 Medium Beige
Grey

― 738 Very Light Tan

C 921 Light Rust

7 919 Medium
Sienna

⸬ 948 Very Light
Peach

■ 813 Light Blue

≡ 353 Peach

‖ 3325 Baby Blue

╱ 818 Baby Pink

V 776 Medium Pink

● 899 Light
Carnation Pink

Z 434 Light Brown

O 436 Tan

Backstitch Hands 353

YOUNG LADY WITH PARASOL

CHILD WITH HOOP AND STICK

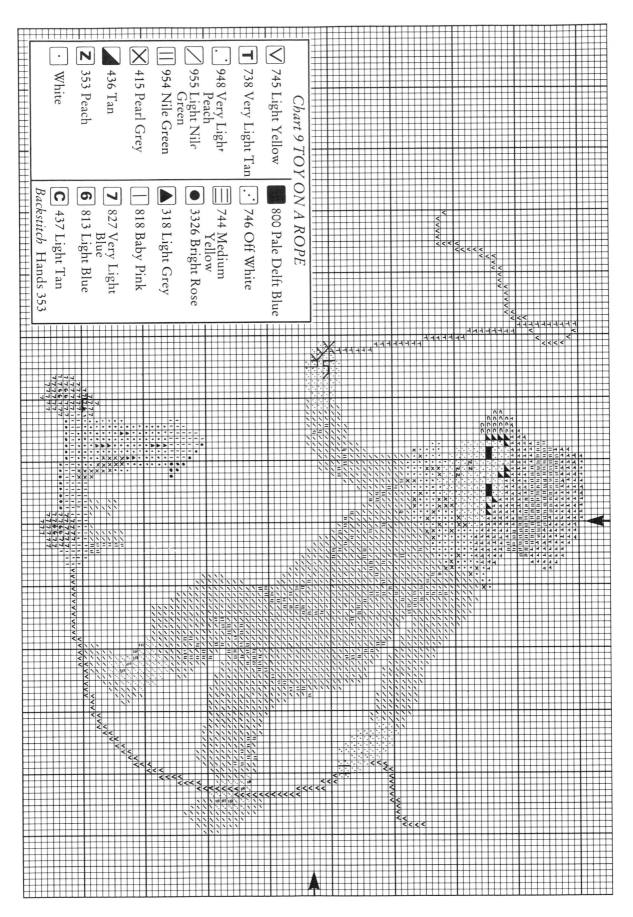

Chart 9 TOY ON A ROPE

Symbol	Colour
V	745 Light Yellow
T	738 Very Light Tan
.	948 Very Light Peach
/	955 Light Nile Green
‖	954 Nile Green
X	415 Pearl Grey
◣	436 Tan
Z	353 Peach
.	White
■	800 Pale Delft Blue
∴	746 Off White
≡	744 Medium Yellow
●	3326 Bright Rose
▲	318 Light Grey
I	818 Baby Pink
7	827 Very Light Blue
6	813 Light Blue
C	437 Light Tan

Backstitch Hands 353

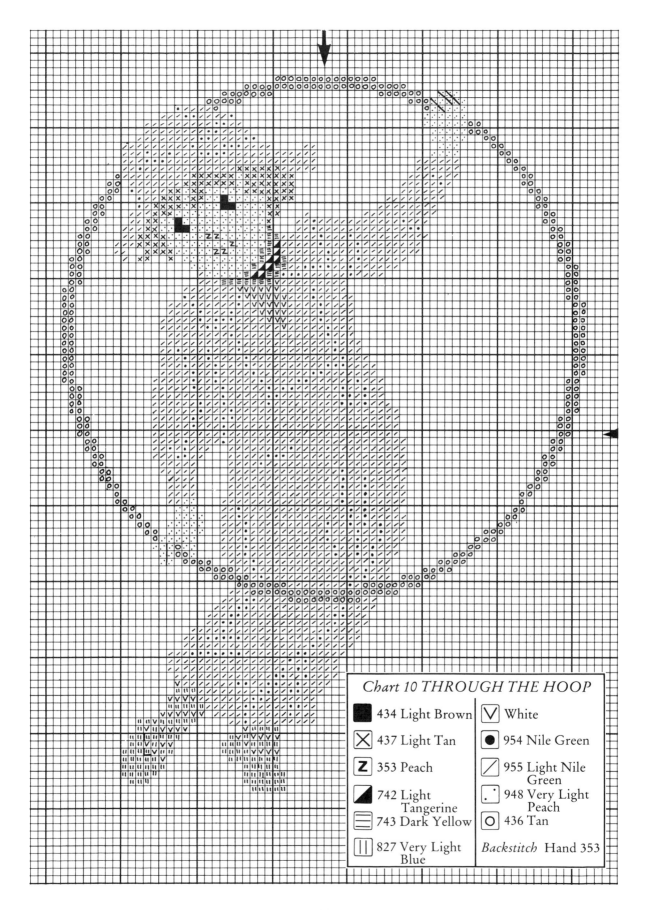

Chart 10 THROUGH THE HOOP

	434 Light Brown	V	White
X	437 Light Tan	●	954 Nile Green
Z	353 Peach	/	955 Light Nile Green
◢	742 Light Tangerine	.·	948 Very Light Peach
=	743 Dark Yellow	O	436 Tan
‖	827 Very Light Blue		

Backstitch Hand 353

TOY ON A ROPE

THROUGH THE HOOP

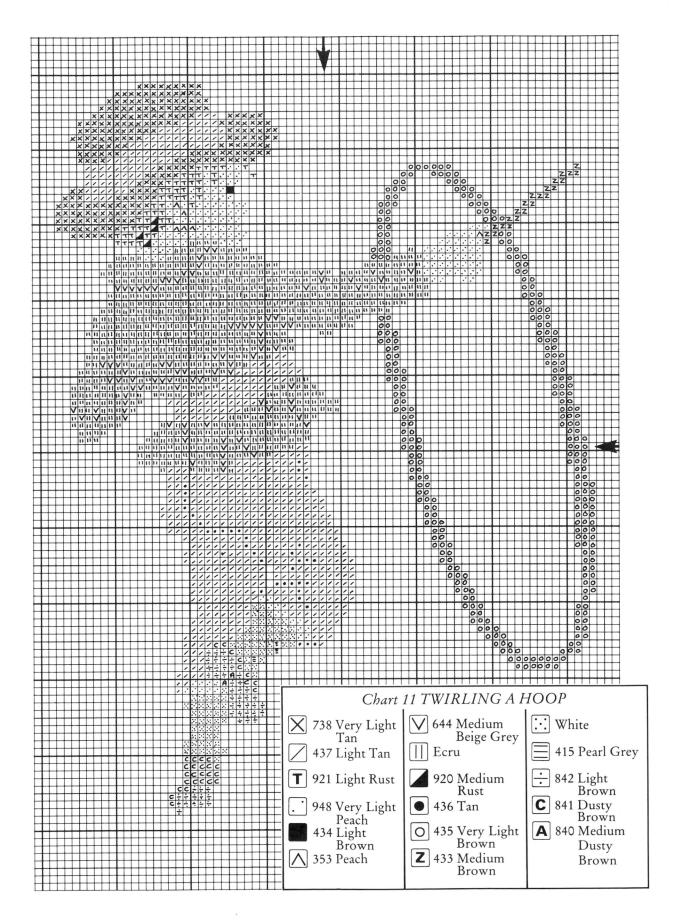

Chart 11 TWIRLING A HOOP

Symbol	Color	Symbol	Color	Symbol	Color
X	738 Very Light Tan	V	644 Medium Beige Grey	∴	White
∕	437 Light Tan	‖	Ecru	☰	415 Pearl Grey
T	921 Light Rust	◢	920 Medium Rust	∴	842 Light Brown
.	948 Very Light Peach	●	436 Tan	C	841 Dusty Brown
■	434 Light Brown	O	435 Very Light Brown	A	840 Medium Dusty Brown
∧	353 Peach	Z	433 Medium Brown		

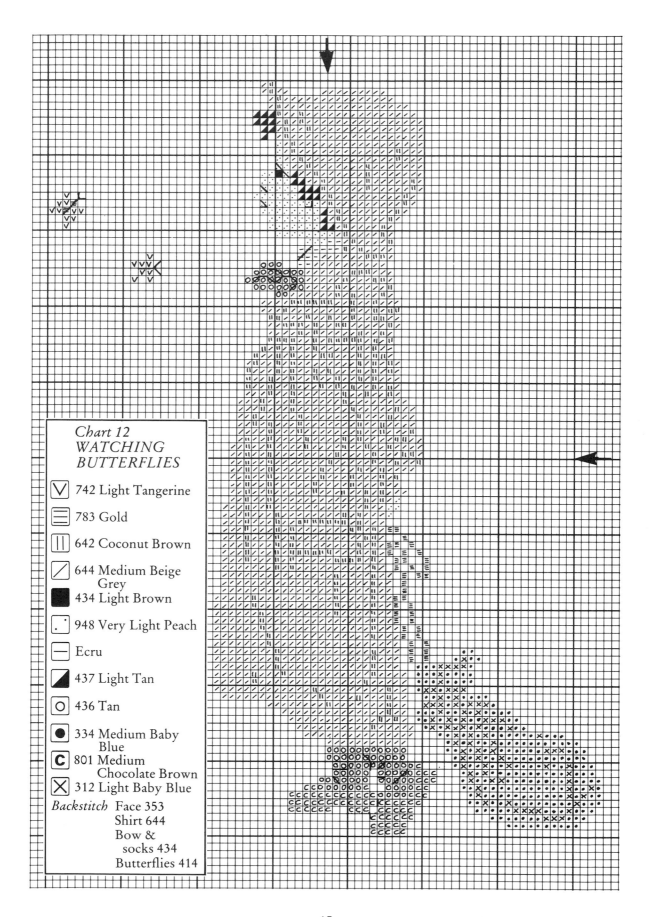

Chart 12
*WATCHING
BUTTERFLIES*

☑	742 Light Tangerine
☰	783 Gold
∥	642 Coconut Brown
╱	644 Medium Beige Grey
■	434 Light Brown
⊡	948 Very Light Peach
⊟	Ecru
◪	437 Light Tan
Ⓞ	436 Tan
●	334 Medium Baby Blue
Ⓒ	801 Medium Chocolate Brown
☒	312 Light Baby Blue

Backstitch Face 353
Shirt 644
Bow &
   socks 434
Butterflies 414

45

TWIRLING A HOOP

WATCHING BUTTERFLIES

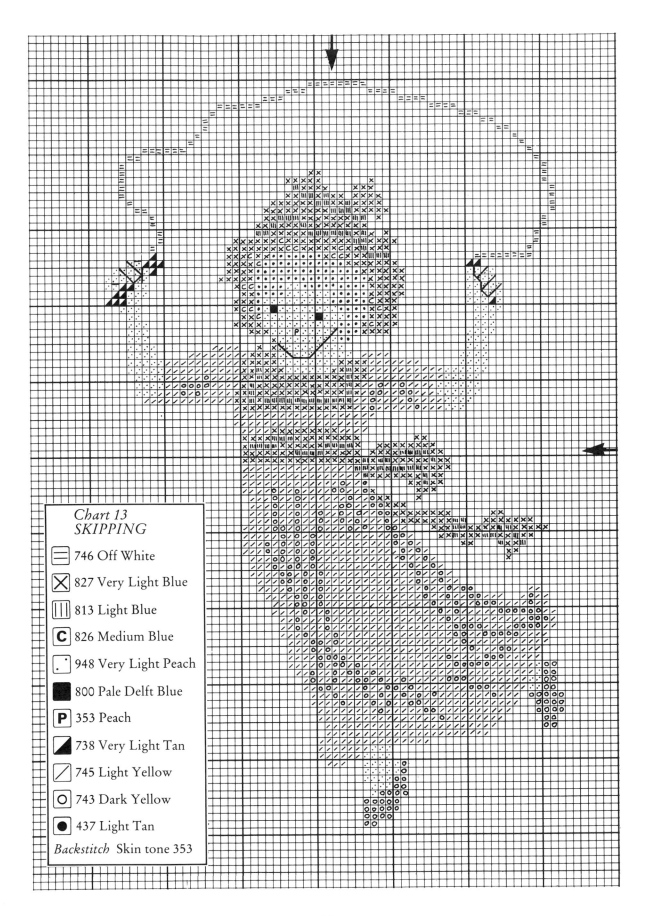

Chart 13
SKIPPING

⚌	746 Off White
✕	827 Very Light Blue
⦀	813 Light Blue
C	826 Medium Blue
⦂	948 Very Light Peach
◼	800 Pale Delft Blue
P	353 Peach
◣	738 Very Light Tan
╱	745 Light Yellow
O	743 Dark Yellow
●	437 Light Tan

Backstitch Skin tone 353

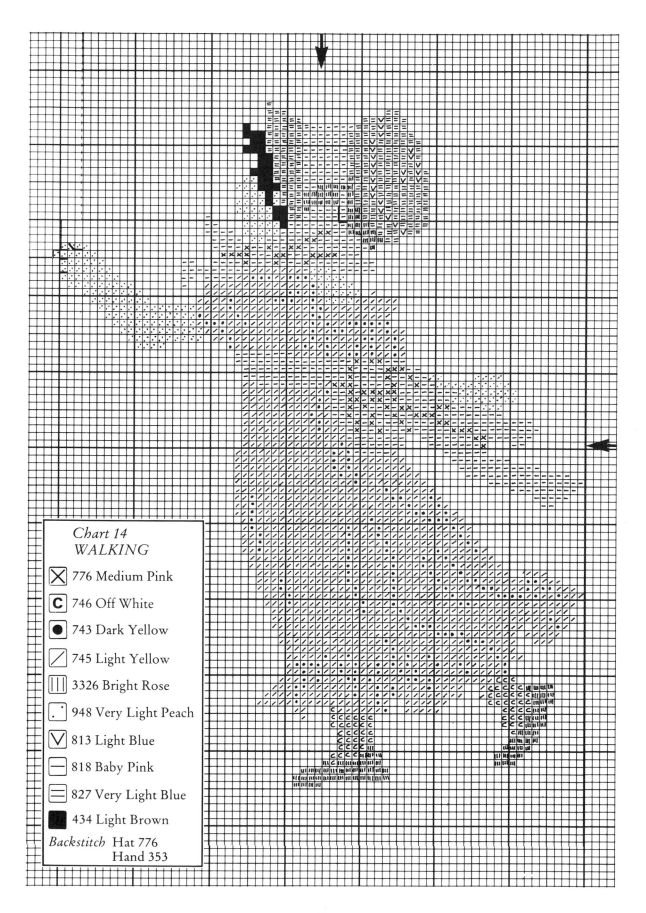

Chart 14
WALKING

☒ 776 Medium Pink

C 746 Off White

● 743 Dark Yellow

╱ 745 Light Yellow

||| 3326 Bright Rose

⋰ 948 Very Light Peach

∨ 813 Light Blue

− 818 Baby Pink

= 827 Very Light Blue

■ 434 Light Brown

Backstitch Hat 776
Hand 353

SKIPPING

WALKING

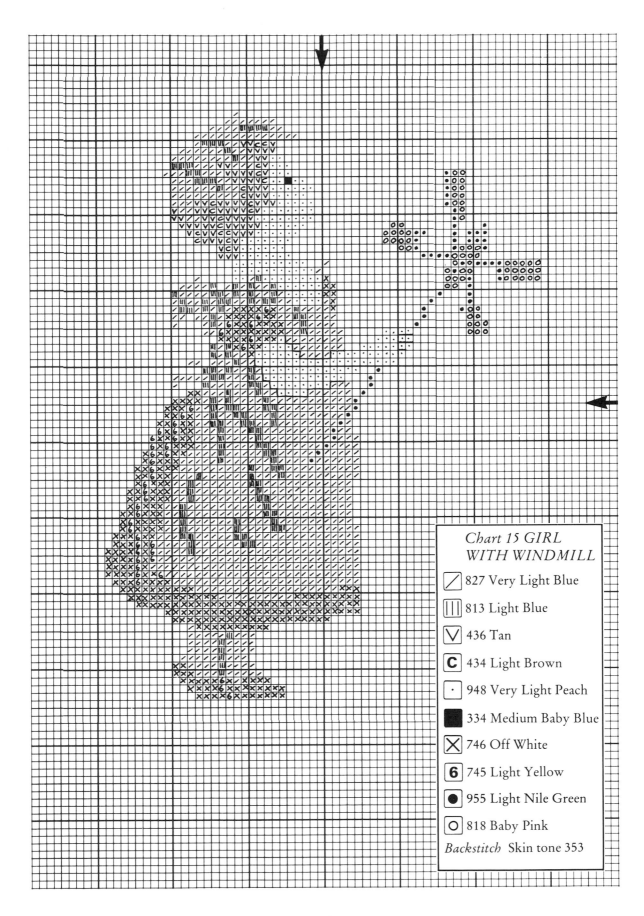

Chart 15 GIRL
WITH WINDMILL

/	827 Very Light Blue
|||	813 Light Blue
V	436 Tan
C	434 Light Brown
·	948 Very Light Peach
■	334 Medium Baby Blue
X	746 Off White
6	745 Light Yellow
●	955 Light Nile Green
O	818 Baby Pink

Backstitch Skin tone 353

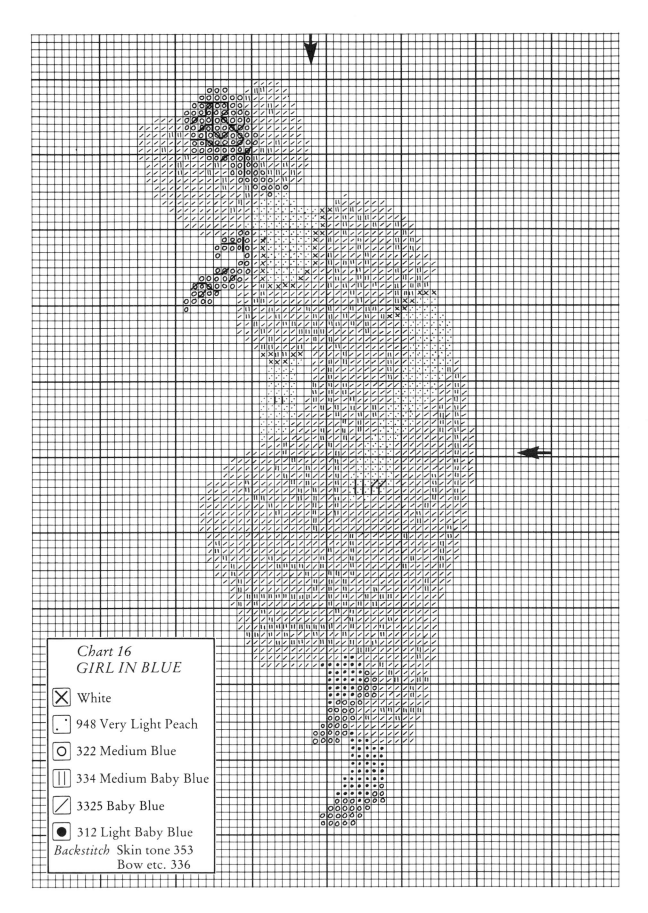

Chart 16
GIRL IN BLUE

|X| White

|.| 948 Very Light Peach

|O| 322 Medium Blue

|||| 334 Medium Baby Blue

|/| 3325 Baby Blue

|●| 312 Light Baby Blue

Backstitch Skin tone 353
            Bow etc. 336

GIRL WITH WINDMILL

GIRL IN BLUE

FRAMED PICTURES

Girls Talk, and Dancing on the Beach
(Charts 17 & 18)

For each picture you will need:
35 x 45.5cm (13¾ x 18in) piece of ecru pearl Aida with 11 stitches to the inch.
30 x 40.5cm (11¾ x 16in) piece of mounting board
Masking tape
DMC 6-strand stranded cotton

Complete the cross-stitch embroidery using three strands of
stranded cotton.

Little Tom Tucker
(Chart 20)

30.5 x 30.5cm (12 x 12in) piece of ecru Ainring with 18 stitches to the inch.
25.5 x 25.5cm (10 x 10in) piece of mounting board
Masking tape
DMC 6-strand stranded cotton

Complete the cross-stitch embroidery using two strands of
stranded cotton.

Little Bo-Peep
(Chart 21)

33.5 x 39.5cm (13¼ x 15½in) piece of sky-blue Ainring with 18 stitches to the inch.
28.5 x 34.5cm (11¼ x 13½in) piece of mounting board
Masking tape
DMC 6-strand stranded cotton

Complete the cross-stitch embroidery using two strands of
stranded cotton.

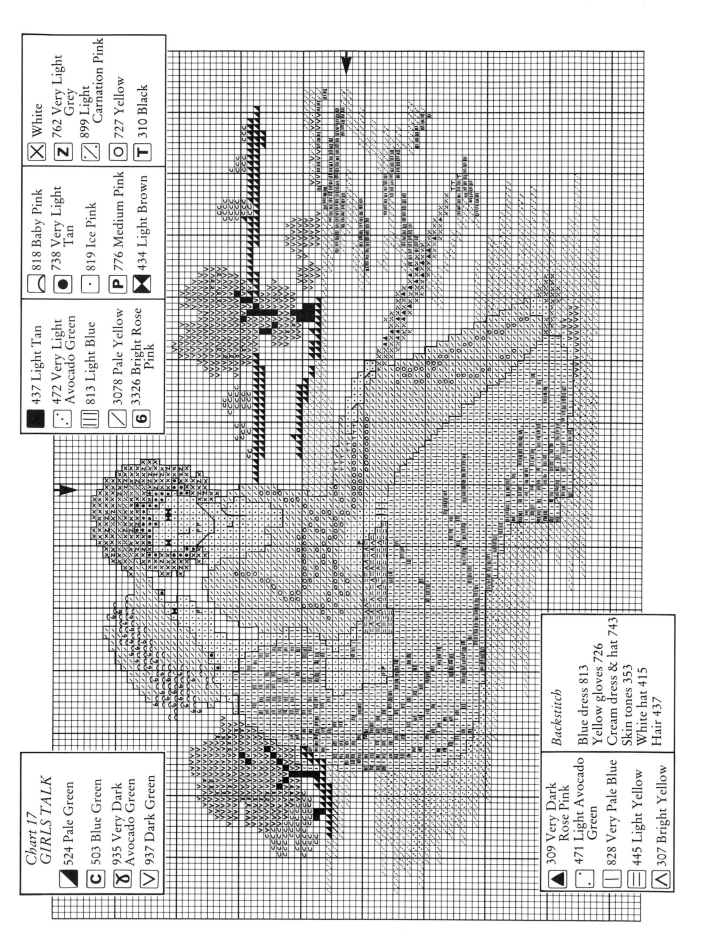

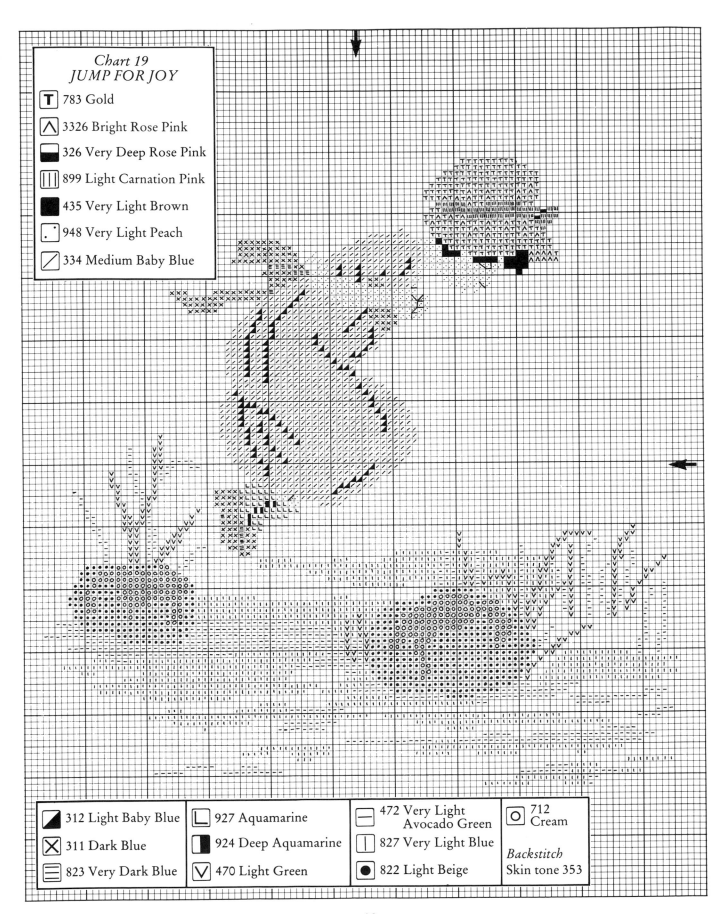

Chart 19
JUMP FOR JOY

- **T** 783 Gold
- **∧** 3326 Bright Rose Pink
- **▬** 326 Very Deep Rose Pink
- **|||** 899 Light Carnation Pink
- **■** 435 Very Light Brown
- **·** 948 Very Light Peach
- **╱** 334 Medium Baby Blue

- **◢** 312 Light Baby Blue
- **✕** 311 Dark Blue
- **≣** 823 Very Dark Blue
- **L** 927 Aquamarine
- **▮** 924 Deep Aquamarine
- **V** 470 Light Green
- **−** 472 Very Light Avocado Green
- **|** 827 Very Light Blue
- **●** 822 Light Beige
- **O** 712 Cream

Backstitch
Skin tone 353

Jump for Joy
(Chart 19)

37 x 39.5cm (14½ x 15½in) piece of white Linda with 27 stitches to the inch.
32 x 34.5cm (12½ x 13½in) piece of mounting board
Masking tape
DMC 6-strand stranded cotton

Complete the cross-stitch embroidery using three strands of stranded cotton, sewing across two squares of the Linda, effectively making it fourteen to the inch.

Polly Flinders and Friends, and Polly and Friends Dancing
(Charts 22 & 23)

For each picture you will need:
41.5 x 47cm (16½ x 18½in) piece of cream fine Aida with 14 stitches to the inch.
36.5 x 42cm (14½ x 16½in) piece of mounting board.
Masking tape
DMC 6-strand stranded cotton.

Complete the cross-stitch embroidery using two strands of stranded cotton.

These projects have more backstitch than the other pictures.
The backstitch colours are shown on the key, alongside their associated main colours.

MOUNTING

When you have completed your cross-stitch embroidery, press it so that it is nice and flat, ready for mounting. Mount your embroidery by stretching it over the mounting board. To do this, place the embroidery face down on to a clean flat surface and place the mounting board centrally on to it. Fold one edge of the fabric over the mounting board (making sure it is perfectly straight) and secure with pins along the edge of the board. Secure the opposite edge in the same way, ensuring that the fabric is straight and taut on the board. Use masking tape to secure the fabric on the back of the mounting board and remove the pins. Repeat this procedure on the remaining two edges.

Your embroidery picture is now ready to be framed. The best result will be achieved if you take it to a professional framer.

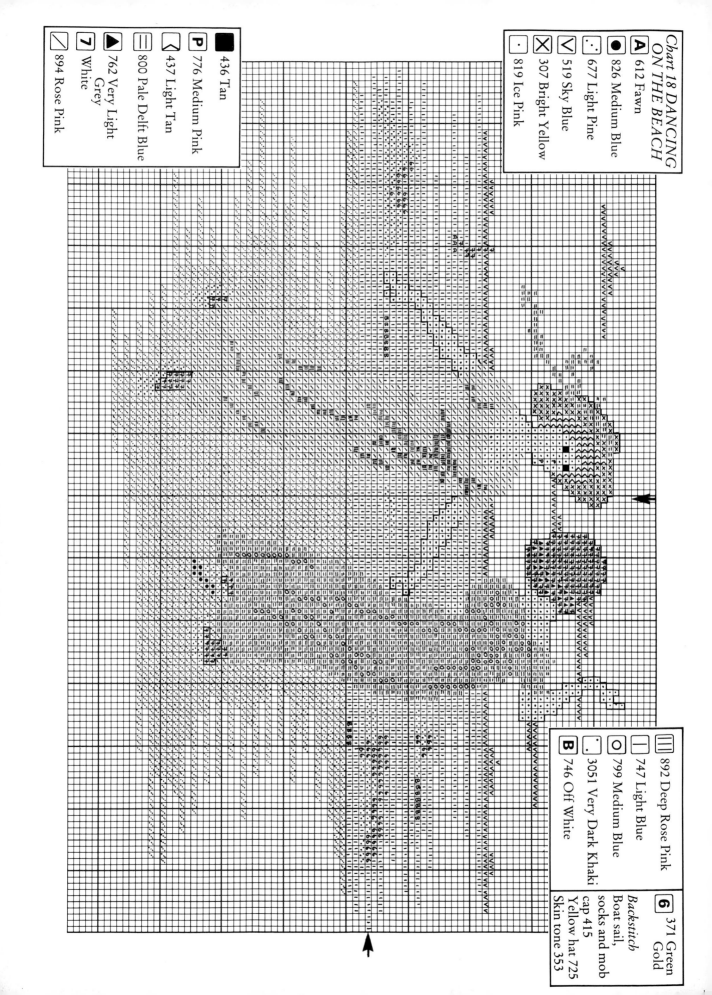

Chart 18 DANCING
ON THE BEACH

	612 Fawn
A	
●	826 Medium Blue
∴	677 Light Pine
V	519 Sky Blue
X	307 Bright Yellow
·	819 Ice Pink

■	436 Tan
P	776 Medium Pink
⟨	437 Light Tan
≡	800 Pale Delft Blue
▲	762 Very Light Grey
7	White
╱	894 Rose Pink

				892 Deep Rose Pink
		747 Light Blue
O	799 Medium Blue
·	3051 Very Dark Khaki
B	746 Off White

| 6 | 371 Green Gold |

Backstitch
Boat sail,
socks and mob
cap
Yellow hat 725
Skin tone 353

Chart 20 LITTLE TOM TUCKER

O	3053 Grey Green	. ˙	828 Very Pale Blue	V	3032 Beige Brown
T	921 Light Rust	|	372 Light Khaki	||	738 Very Light Tan
·	948 Very Light Peach	X	778 Light Antique Mauve		*Backstitch*
Y	352 Medium Peach	☰	316 Medium Antique Mauve		Gate 370
.˙	White	Z	320 Medium Pistachio Green		Flowers 319
■	827 Very Light Blue	C	966 Pale Green		Hat 3051
—	813 Light Blue	◣	223 Medium Old Rose		Skin tone 352
					Suit 518
					Collar 414
					Lettering 370

64

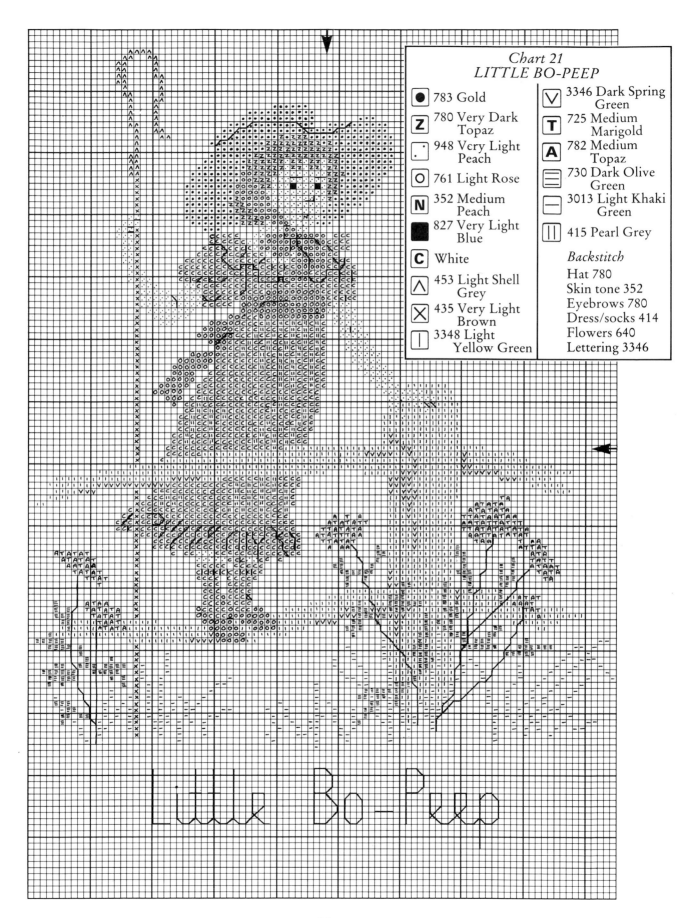

Chart 21
LITTLE BO-PEEP

Symbol	Color	Symbol	Color
●	783 Gold	V	3346 Dark Spring Green
Z	780 Very Dark Topaz	T	725 Medium Marigold
·	948 Very Light Peach	A	782 Medium Topaz
O	761 Light Rose	≡	730 Dark Olive Green
N	352 Medium Peach	−	3013 Light Khaki Green
■	827 Very Light Blue	‖	415 Pearl Grey
C	White		
∧	453 Light Shell Grey		
X	435 Very Light Brown		
‖	3348 Light Yellow Green		

Backstitch
Hat 780
Skin tone 352
Eyebrows 780
Dress/socks 414
Flowers 640
Lettering 3346

Little Tom Tucker

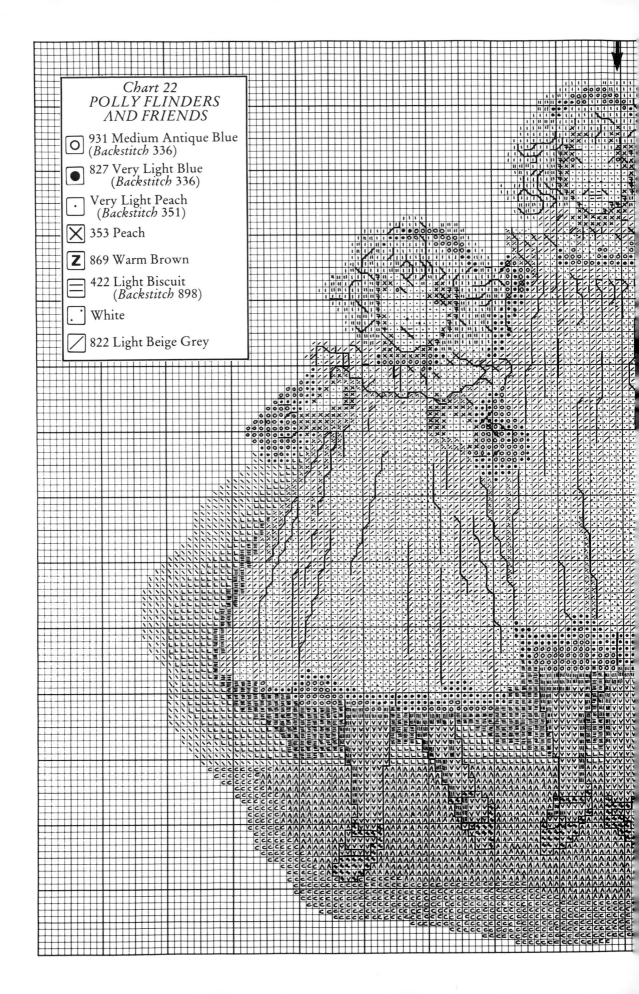

Chart 22
POLLY FLINDERS
AND FRIENDS

⊙ 931 Medium Antique Blue
   (*Backstitch* 336)

● 827 Very Light Blue
   (*Backstitch* 336)

· Very Light Peach
   (*Backstitch* 351)

☒ 353 Peach

Z 869 Warm Brown

≡ 422 Light Biscuit
   (*Backstitch* 898)

· White

╱ 822 Light Beige Grey

644 Medium Beige Grey
(*Backstitch* 640)

677 Light Pine

3046 Medium Yellow Beige
(*Backstitch* 680, eyebrows & hair)

352 Medium Peach

351 Coral

648 Light Beaver Grey

646 Grey (backstitch 844)

645 Dark Pewter Grey

3024 Very Light Brown Grey

3023 Light Brown Grey

3022 Medium Brown Grey

950 Medium Flesh

407 Light Brown

758 Light Dusty Rose

356 Melon Pink (*Backstitch* 355)

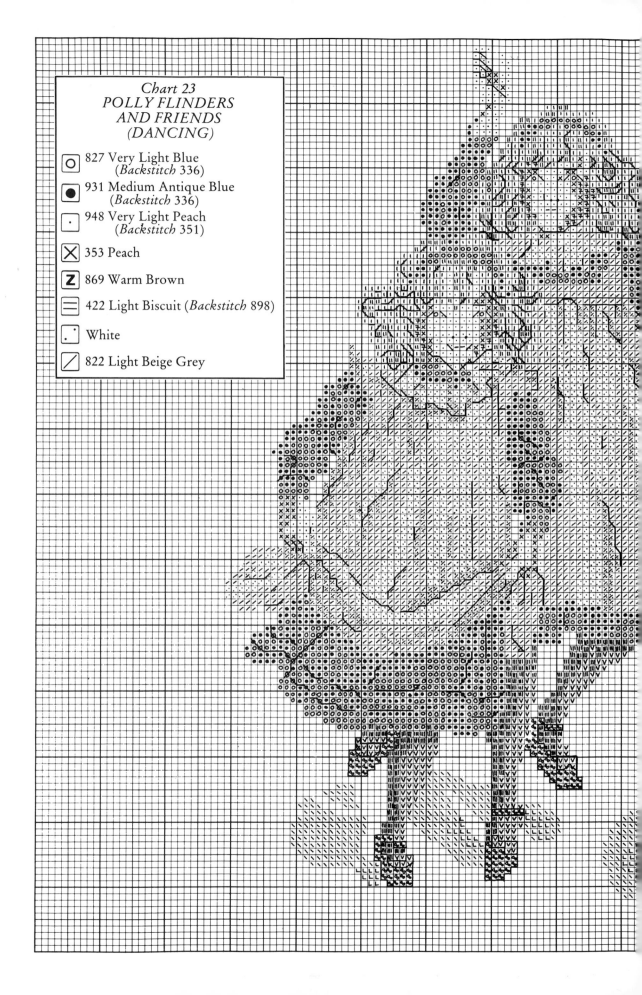

Chart 23
POLLY FLINDERS
AND FRIENDS
(DANCING)

O 827 Very Light Blue
(*Backstitch* 336)

● 931 Medium Antique Blue
(*Backstitch* 336)

· 948 Very Light Peach
(*Backstitch* 351)

X 353 Peach

Z 869 Warm Brown

= 422 Light Biscuit (*Backstitch* 898)

· White

/ 822 Light Beige Grey

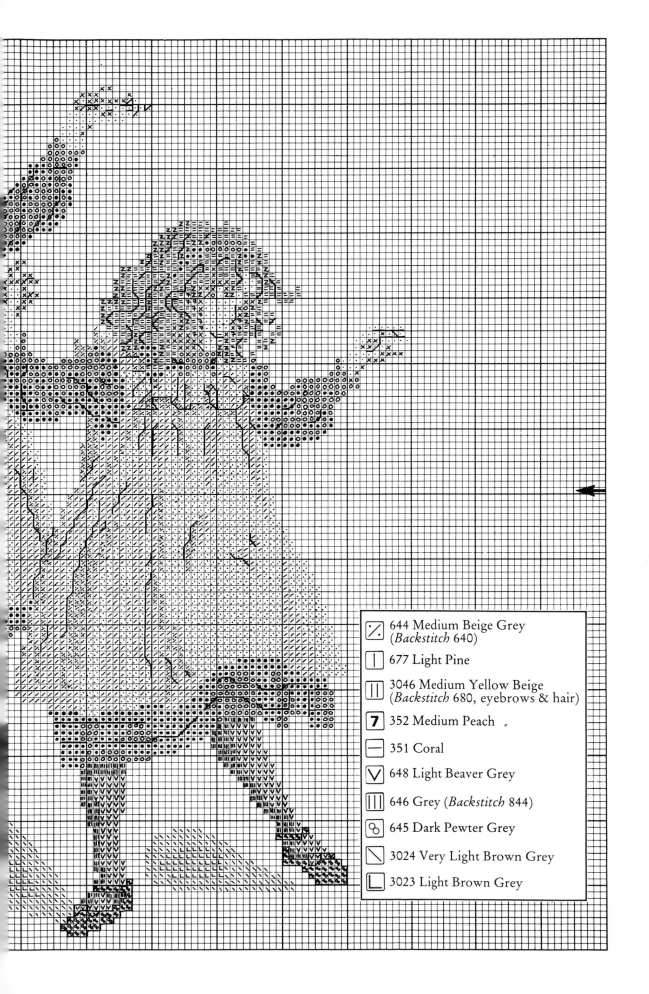

	644 Medium Beige Grey (*Backstitch* 640)
	677 Light Pine
	3046 Medium Yellow Beige (*Backstitch* 680, eyebrows & hair)
7	352 Medium Peach
	351 Coral
V	648 Light Beaver Grey
	646 Grey (*Backstitch* 844)
℗	645 Dark Pewter Grey
	3024 Very Light Brown Grey
L	3023 Light Brown Grey

LAVENDER BAGS

A dainty lace-trimmed lavender bag is far too pretty to be hidden away inside your wardrobe. Try hanging it on a handle or even on the bed-post to make your bedroom smell fragrant. This pensive pair is sewn on a sky-blue background for an unusual and striking effect. (Charts 24 & 25)

MATERIALS
For each bag you will need:
17 x 17cm (6¾ x 6¾in) square of sky-blue Ainring with 18 stitches per inch
17 x 17cm (6¾ x 6¾in) square of sky-blue fabric for the backing
(These measurements include a 12mm (½in) seam allowance)
50cm (19¾in) white ribbon 6mm (¼in) wide
70cm (27½in) white lace 2cm (1in) wide
Small bag of kapok
Small amount of lavender
Adhesive
DMC 6-strand stranded cotton
Sewing thread to match the fabric

DIRECTIONS
Complete your cross-stitch embroidery centrally on the Ainring using two strands of stranded cotton. When completed, press flat.

Making up the bag

1 Pin the ribbon and lace on to the Ainring just over the stitching line and tack.

2 Place the backing material on to the Ainring, right sides together. Pin and tack.

3 Either machine- or hand-stitch together, leaving an opening on one side of about 4cm (1½in) for turning.

4 Remove the pins and tacking stitches and turn to the right side.

5 Use a scrap piece of backing material to make a lavender sachet. Place this inside the bag and fix it to the wrong side of the Ainring using a small amount of adhesive.

6 Fill the bag with kapok, using small amounts at a time to get an even filling.
Hand-stitch the opening closed.

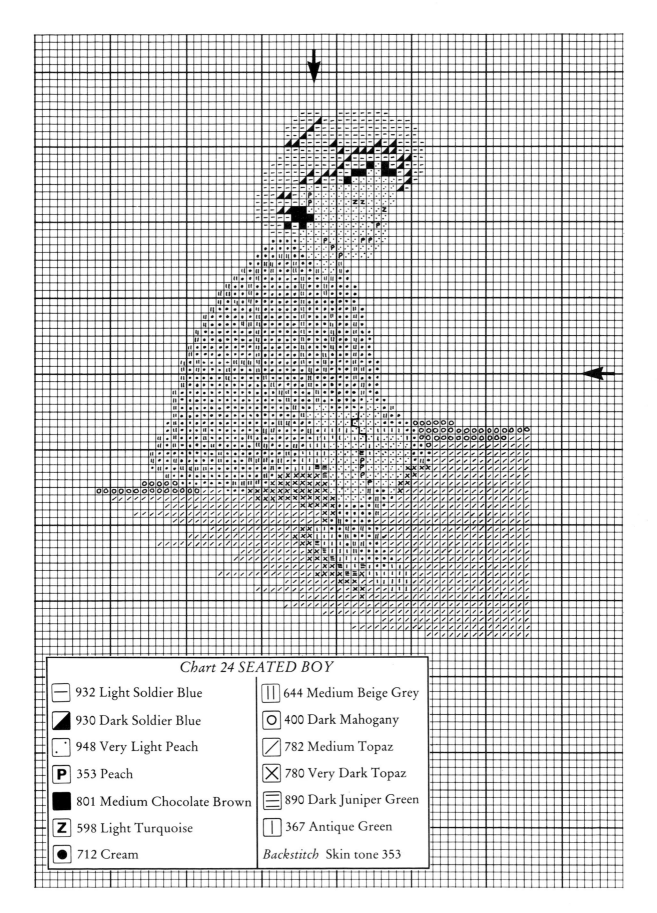

Chart 24 SEATED BOY

	932 Light Soldier Blue		644 Medium Beige Grey
	930 Dark Soldier Blue		400 Dark Mahogany
	948 Very Light Peach		782 Medium Topaz
P	353 Peach		780 Very Dark Topaz
	801 Medium Chocolate Brown		890 Dark Juniper Green
Z	598 Light Turquoise		367 Antique Green
	712 Cream	*Backstitch* Skin tone 353

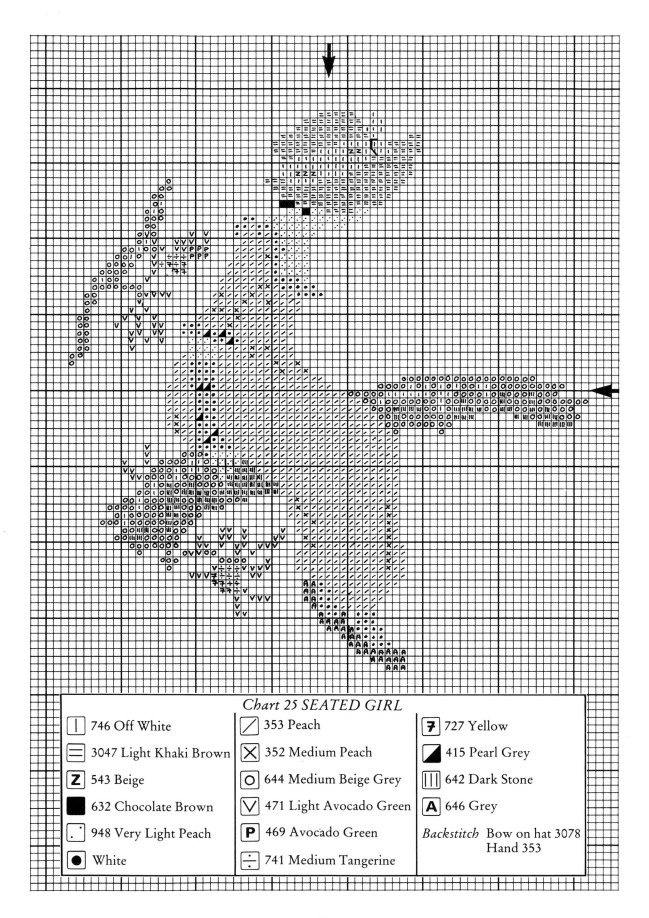

Chart 25 SEATED GIRL

⏐ 746 Off White	∕ 353 Peach	7 727 Yellow
═ 3047 Light Khaki Brown	✕ 352 Medium Peach	◣ 415 Pearl Grey
Z 543 Beige	○ 644 Medium Beige Grey	⦀ 642 Dark Stone
■ 632 Chocolate Brown	✓ 471 Light Avocado Green	A 646 Grey
∴ 948 Very Light Peach	P 469 Avocado Green	*Backstitch* Bow on hat 3078
● White	÷ 741 Medium Tangerine	Hand 353

GREETINGS CARDS

These designs are quick to sew and make a charming, personalised alternative to buying a card. A cross-stitch gift such as a paperweight or lavender bag could be combined with a cross-stitch card, for an original gift. (Chart 26)

MATERIALS
DMC special occasion cards:

Girl in White: pink card with 9 x 5cm (3½ x 2in) rectangular cut-out
Circle Design: white card with 6cm (2½in) round cut-out
Boy in Suit: blue card with 11 x 8cm (4½ x 3in) rectangular cut-out
Small Child: white card with 8 x 5cm (3 x 2in) oval cut-out
Girl in Pink: blue card with 10 x 8cm (4 x 3in) oval cut-out
Kite: white card with 10 x 5cm (3 x 2in) oval cut-out

White Hardanger with 22 stitches to the inch for all designs except the kite
Cream Hardanger with 22 stitches to the inch for the kite
DMC 6-strand stranded cotton
Double-sided adhesive tape

DIRECTIONS
To economise on fabric, cut a piece large enough to sew on several designs (remembering to space them well), rather than cutting a small piece for each design.
Complete the cross-stitch embroidery using one strand of stranded cotton. When you have completed the cross-stitch embroideries, centralise the design in the card 'window' and trim the fabric to fit.
Use double-sided tape to fix the design into the card and press the backing down firmly (see the diagram).

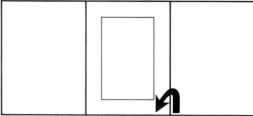

Fig 7 MAKING UP THE GREETINGS CARDS

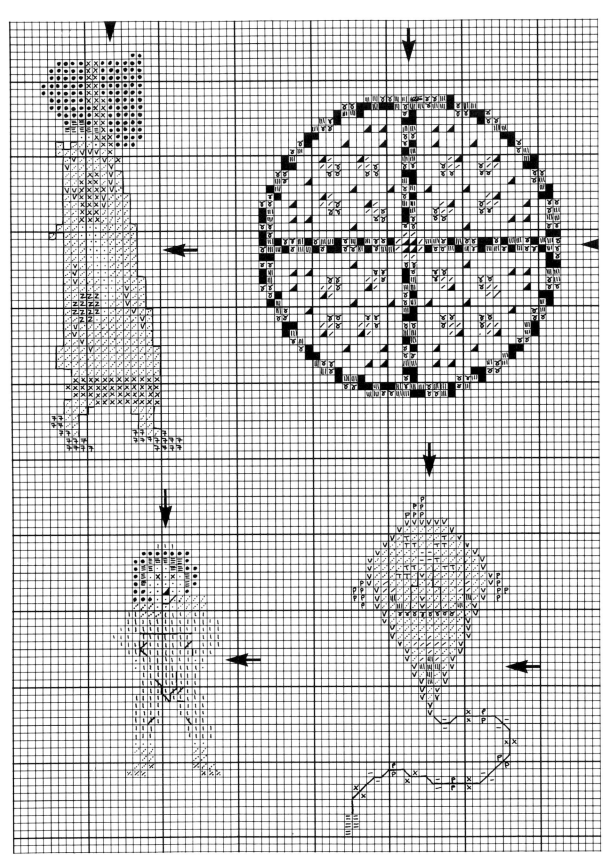

Chart 26a GIRL IN WHITE, CIRCLE DESIGN, SMALL CHILD, KITE

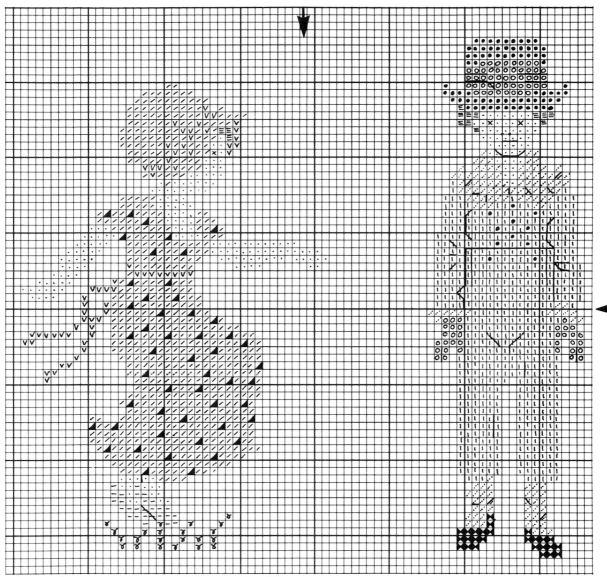

Chart 26b GIRL IN PINK, BOY IN SUIT

Chart 26a, b		
ɣ 703 Chartreuse	V 415 Pearl Grey	T 318 Light Grey
‖‖ 701 Light Christmas Green	X 813 Light Blue	— 3326 Bright Rose
■ 699 Christmas Green	ǀ 3325 Baby Blue	= 807 Peacock Blue
/ 776 Medium Pink	O 317 Pewter Grey	
◢ 899 Light Carnation Pink	◪ 3041 Antique Mauve	*Backstitch* Skin tones 352
● 738 Very Light Tan	Z 335 Medium Pink	White dress, suit collar
· 948 Very Light Peach	7 840 Medium Dusty Brown	& socks 415
= 921 Light Rust	⟋ 437 Light Tan	Gloves & hat 310
∴ White	P 744 Medium Yellow	Suits 334
		Pink shoes 335
		Windmill 415
		Kite string 3023

MINIATURES

These delightful miniature pictures will make an attractive addition to your home, whether they are displayed singly or together. Any one of the five designs would make a lovely present. (Charts 27 & 28)

MATERIALS
DMC miniature frames as follows:

Boy and Girl, Girl Seated: 15cm (6in) round in brass
Windmill: 8cm (3in) round in brass
Two Boys: 10cm (4in) round in brass
Small Boy: 6 x 9cm (2½ x 3½in) oval in brass

Fine Aida with 14 stitches per inch (the colours chosen were cream, sage and lemon)
DMC 6-strand stranded cotton

DIRECTIONS
Use two strands of the stranded cotton to sew up your designs. When you have completed the cross-stitch embroideries, gently remove all parts of the frame and use the template provided to draw around your design, ensuring that it is central.

Next, place the clear acetate into the frame, followed by your embroidery, then the thin card followed by the backing.

Your frame is now complete.

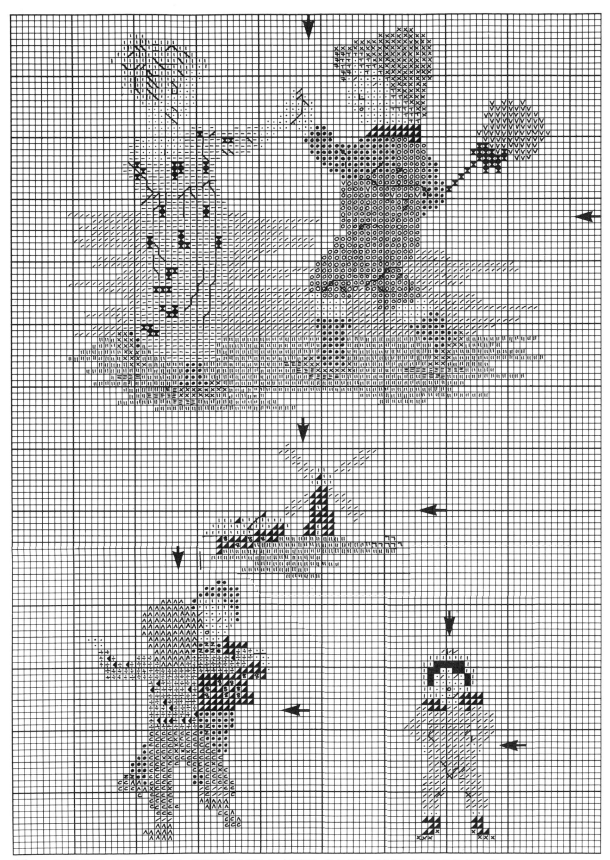

Chart 27 BOY AND GIRL, WINDMILL, TWO BOYS, AND SMALL BOY

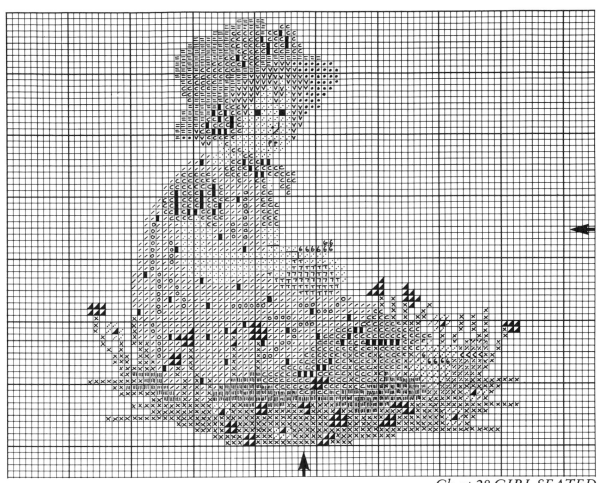

Chart 28 GIRL SEATED

Chart 27	
⊡ 948 Very Light Peach	— 676 Light Old Gold
‖ 472 Very Light Avocado Green	⊓ 581 Khaki
≡ 471 Light Avocado Green	⊗ 415 Pearl Grey
⁄ 827 Very Light Blue	Z 517 Rich Blue
O 353 Peach	∧ 413 Charcoal Grey
● 518 Medium Blue	÷ 922 Light Rust
X 436 Tan	◀ 920 Medium Rust
7 434 Light Brown	C 422 Light Biscuit
◤ White	■ 610 Brown
V 744 Medium Yellow	*Backstitch*
T 739 Light Tan	All skin tones 353
⫿ 738 Very Light Tan	Girl's hair 436
⊠ 470 Light Green	Girl's dress 471
	Boy's suit 351
	Roof 436
	Child's suit etc, 826
	If required, outline any white areas with 415

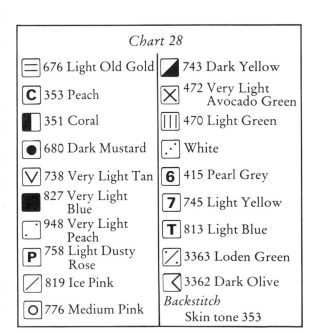

Chart 28	
≡ 676 Light Old Gold	◣ 743 Dark Yellow
C 353 Peach	X 472 Very Light Avocado Green
■ 351 Coral	‖ 470 Light Green
● 680 Dark Mustard	⫶ White
V 738 Very Light Tan	6 415 Pearl Grey
■ 827 Very Light Blue	7 745 Light Yellow
⫶ 948 Very Light Peach	T 813 Light Blue
P 758 Light Dusty Rose	⁄ 3363 Loden Green
⁄ 819 Ice Pink	◀ 3362 Dark Olive
O 776 Medium Pink	*Backstitch*
	Skin tone 353

TABLECLOTH

A tablecloth is a good way of displaying your cross-stitch expertise, and always makes a welcome gift. Used at home, this lovely tablecloth will be admired by everyone for its delicate Kate Greenaway motifs. (Charts 29 & 30)

MATERIALS
1m (39½in) cream Hardida
DMC 6-stranded cotton
Sewing thread to match the fabric

DIRECTIONS

The tablecloth is worked on Hardida which is a checkerboard fabric consisting of 8cm (3¼in) squares, alternating between Aida and Hardanger.
The finished cloth measures 94 x 94cm (37 x 37in), so you will need to cut your fabric to measure 98 x 98cm (38½ x 38½in) to allow for hemming. When you cut the fabric, ensure that you begin and end with a Hardanger square.

Begin the cross-stitch embroidery on the second row of squares using one strand of the stranded cotton. Arrange the design so that all four sides of the cloth are the same, placing the circle motif p96 (not the garland) in the centre square (see the diagram as a guide to positioning the motifs).
When you have completed the embroideries, mitre the corners of the tablecloth and hem them all around.

Chart 29 TABLECLOTH MOTIFS

⊟ 921 Light Rust	◪ 415 Pearl Grey	● 738 Very Light Tan
◼ 699 Christmas Green	▯ 827 Very Light Blue	Z 436 Tan
⦀ 701 Light Christmas Green	☒ 813 Light Blue	V 826 Medium Blue
४ 703 Chartreuse	· 948 Very Light Peach	*Backstitch* Ribbon on garland 334
◣ 899 Light Carnation Pink	∴ 818 Baby Pink	Skin tone on girl & boy 761
⁄ 776 Medium Pink	C White	

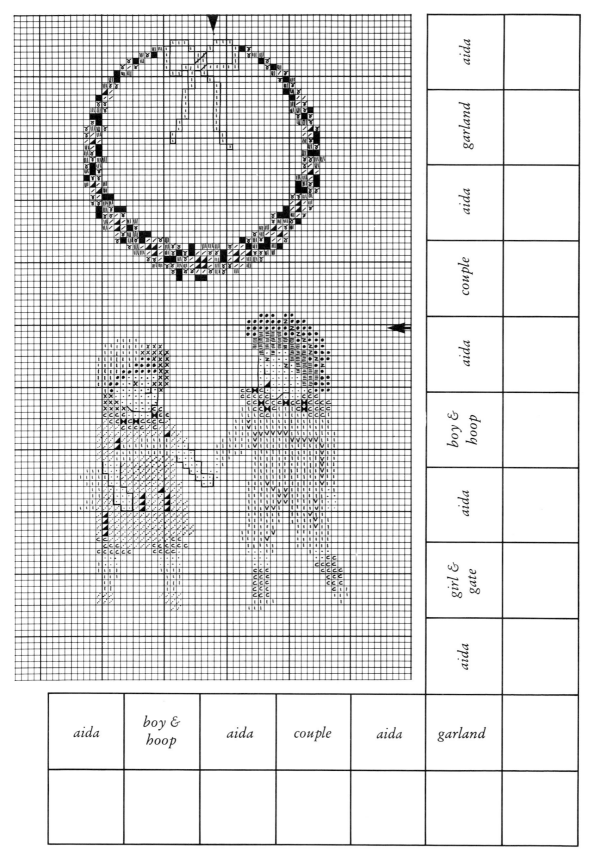

	aida
	garland
	aida
	couple
	aida
	boy & hoop
	aida
	girl & gate
	aida

aida	boy & hoop	aida	couple	aida	garland	

POSITIONING THE MOTIFS ON THE TABLECLOTH

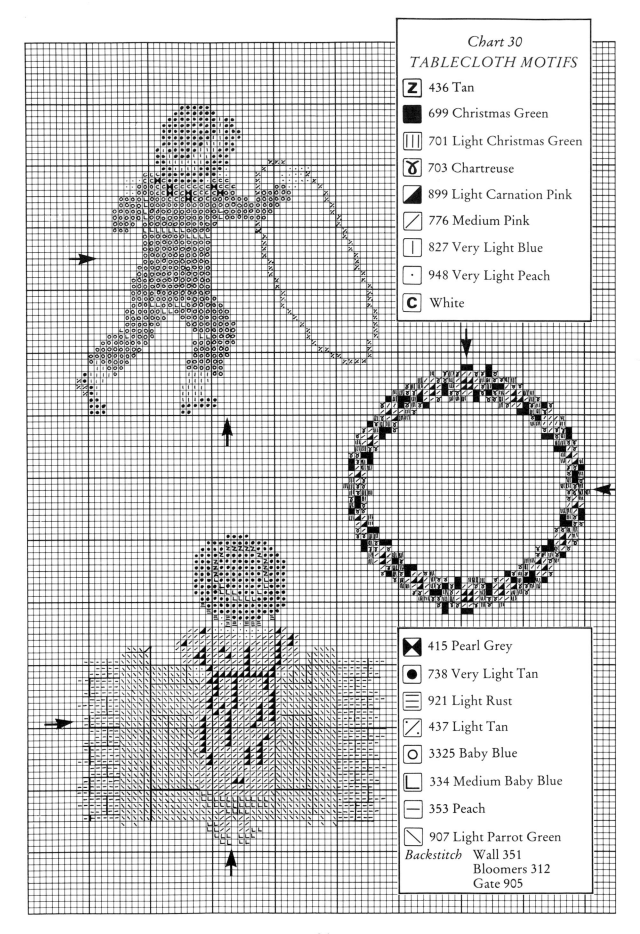

Chart 30
TABLECLOTH MOTIFS

Z	436 Tan
■	699 Christmas Green
⦀	701 Light Christmas Green
8	703 Chartreuse
◣	899 Light Carnation Pink
╱	776 Medium Pink
⎮	827 Very Light Blue
·	948 Very Light Peach
C	White

✕	415 Pearl Grey
●	738 Very Light Tan
≡	921 Light Rust
╱	437 Light Tan
O	3325 Baby Blue
L	334 Medium Baby Blue
−	353 Peach
╲	907 Light Parrot Green

Backstitch   Wall 351
Bloomers 312
Gate 905

JAM-POT COVERS

Use these easily made pretty covers to brighten up your breakfast- or tea-table. (Chart 31)

MATERIALS

White Linda with 27 stitches to the inch
Suitable fabric for backing (cotton, gingham, etc)
Narrow white lace for edging
White ribbon 6mm (¼in) wide
DMC 6-strand stranded cotton
White sewing cotton

DIRECTIONS

Complete the cross-stitch embroideries using two strands of the stranded cotton, sewing across two squares of the Linda, effectively making it 14 to the inch.

1 Measure the diameter of your jam-pot lid and add 6cm (2¼in) for seam allowances.

2 Cut a paper template circle to this diameter.

3 Ensure that the cross-stitch design is centralised, place the template over and cut out circles.

4 Cut circles of backing fabric to the same size.

5 Place right sides together and stitch 6mm (¼in) seam around the outer edge, leaving 19mm (¾in) opening.

6 Trim the seams and turn to the right side. Press flat.

7 Stitch a top seam all round 12mm (½in) from the outer edge.

8 Stitch narrow lace to the outer edge, making sure that you do not close the opening.

9 Thread the ribbon through this hem.

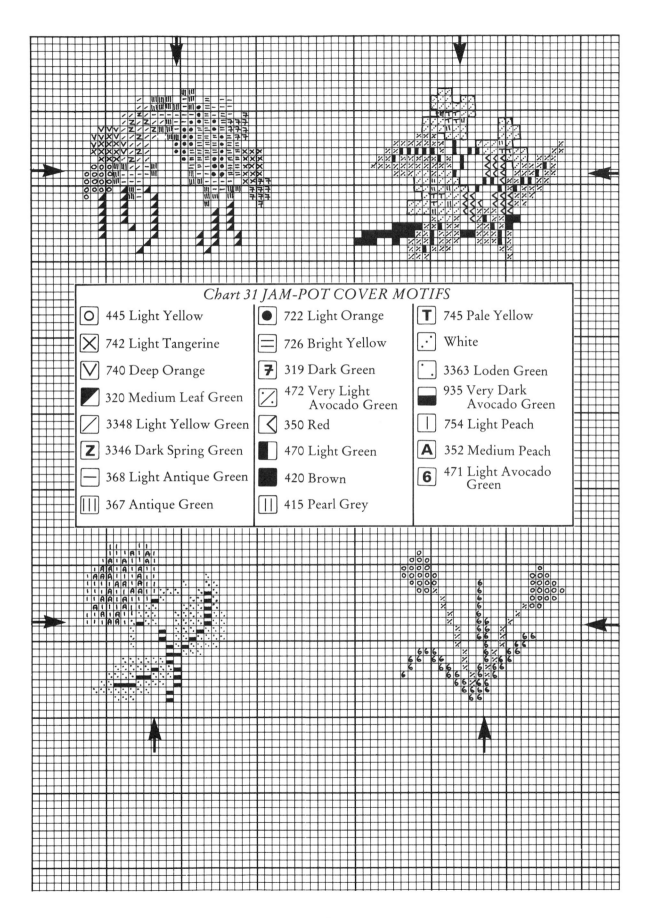

Chart 31 JAM-POT COVER MOTIFS

Symbol	Colour	Symbol	Colour	Symbol	Colour
O	445 Light Yellow	●	722 Light Orange	T	745 Pale Yellow
X	742 Light Tangerine	=	726 Bright Yellow	.·	White
V	740 Deep Orange	7	319 Dark Green	·.	3363 Loden Green
◤	320 Medium Leaf Green	/	472 Very Light Avocado Green	▬	935 Very Dark Avocado Green
/	3348 Light Yellow Green	<	350 Red			754 Light Peach
Z	3346 Dark Spring Green	▌	470 Light Green	A	352 Medium Peach
—	368 Light Antique Green	■	420 Brown	6	471 Light Avocado Green
|||	367 Antique Green	||	415 Pearl Grey		

TRINKET BOXES

Porcelain trinket boxes make beautiful gifts which are both useful and decorative. They can be used to adorn a dressing-table, small table or even a mantelpiece. A trinket box makes an ideal birthday present or even just to thank someone special. (Chart 32)

MATERIALS
DMC trinket boxes:

38mm (1½in) round porcelain trinket box in ivory (circular motif)
76mm (3in) round porcelain trinket box in pink (boy with hoop)
89 x 63mm (3½ x 2½in) oval porcelain trinket box in blue (girl in yellow)

Beige Lugana with 25 stitches per inch for circular motif
White Hardanger with 22 stitches per inch for boy and girl motifs
DMC 6-strand stranded cotton

DIRECTIONS
Complete the cross-stitch embroideries using one strand of stranded cotton.

Place the finished cross-stitch embroidery face up on a firm, flat surface. Gently remove all parts from the trinket-box lid.

Use the rim of the lid to centralise the design. When the design is centralised, draw around the outer edge on to the fabric. Remove the lid and cut the fabric to size.

To assemble the lid, replace the clear acetate and place your design centrally into the lid, with the right side to the acetate. Place the sponge behind your design. Push the metal locking disc very firmly into place using thumb pressure, with the raised side of the disc facing the sponge. When the locking disc is tightly in position, remove the protective film and, if preferred, stick the lid liner to the lid.

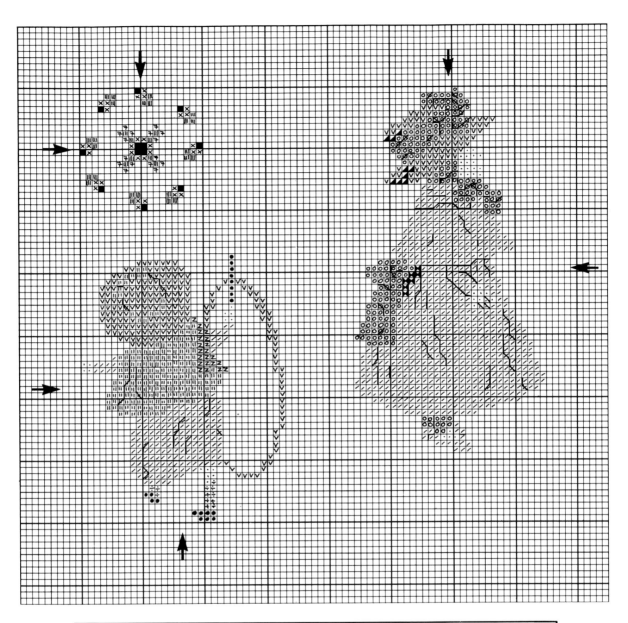

Chart 32 CIRCULAR MOTIF, BOY WITH HOOP, GIRL IN YELLOW

·	948 Very Light Peach	◪	935 Very Dark Avocado Green	*Backstitch*	(Boy with hoop)
╱	727 Yellow	●	436 Tan		Hat 436
◣	437 Light Tan	‖	800 Pale Delft Blue		Bow 799
V	738 Very Light Tan	Z	799 Medium Blue		Skirt 725
O	469 Avocado Green	÷	775 Light Blue		Cape 799

Backstitch (Boy with hoop)
Hat 436
Bow 799
Skirt 725
Cape 799
(Girl)
Bow & socks 935
Dress 725
Skin 352

PAPERWEIGHTS

These pretty paperweights make an unusual gift. They can be put to practical use on a desk or be used as ornaments around the home. (Chart 33)

MATERIALS
DMC paperweights:

9cm (3½in) round paperweight (Garland)
9cm (3½in) fluted paperweight (Child Kneeling)

White Hardanger with 22 stitches per inch
DMC 6-strand stranded cotton

DIRECTIONS
Complete the embroidery using one strand of stranded cotton.
Place the completed embroidery on a firm, flat surface and use the paper template (provided with the paperweight) to draw around your design, ensuring that it is central.
Cut the fabric to size and place right side down into the recess on the base of the paperweight. Place the paper template on to the reverse side of your embroidery. Next, peel the backing off the protective base and very carefully stick it to the base of the paperweight, ensuring that the embroidery and template do not move out of place.

Chart 33 GARLAND, CHILD KNEELING

■	699 Christmas Green	II	762 Very Light Grey
≡	701 Light Christmas Green	I	993 Turquoise
7	704 Medium Apple Green	⁄	739 Light Tan
X	605 Bright Pink	◪	800 Pale Delft Blue
◣	335 Medium Rose Pink	◁	433 Medium Brown
V	738 Very Light Tan		
·	948 Very Light Peach		
O	White		

Backstitch
Skin tone 352
Socks & collar 415
Hat 318
Suit 991

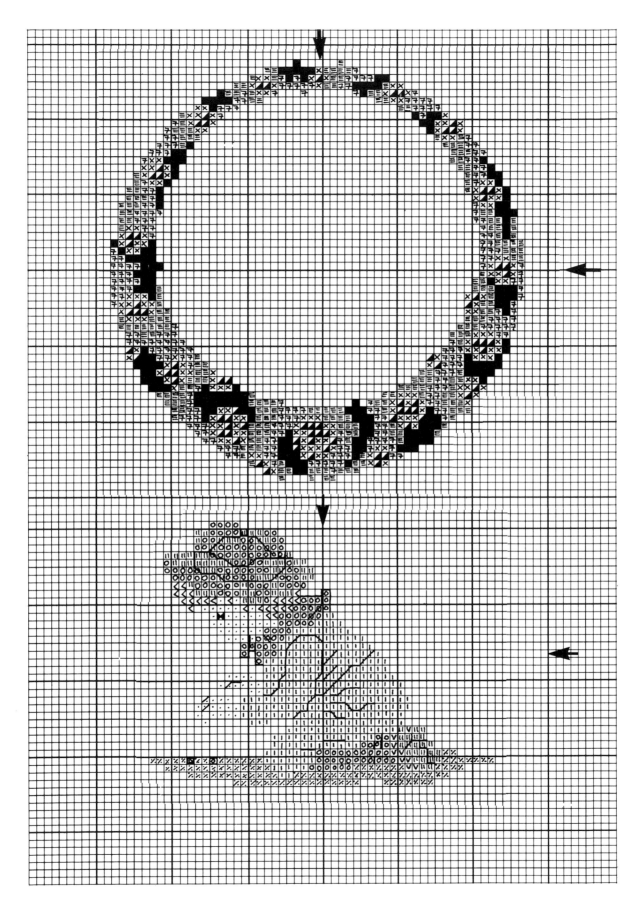

NIGHTDRESS BAG

This useful nightdress bag makes an extremely practical gift. It will be an attractive feature in the bedroom and is suitable for children of any age group. The bag has a draw-string top and is large enough to hold a child's long nightdress or a pair of pyjamas. Alternatively, it can be used as a toy- or shoe-bag. (Charts 34 & 35)

MATERIALS
2m (78¾in) baby blue ribbon 2.5cm (1in) wide
2 pieces sky-blue pearl Aida with 11 stitches to the inch,
measuring approximately 54.5 x 46cm (21½ x 18in)
2 pieces sky-blue lining fabric measuring 49.5 x 40.5cm (19½ x 16in)
DMC 6-strand stranded cotton
Pale blue sewing cotton to match fabric

DIRECTIONS
Complete the cross-stitch picture for the front of the bag using three strands of stranded cotton. Complete the poem for the back of the bag in backstitch using two strands of stranded cotton (796). Cut the pearl Aida to size 49.5 x 40.5cm (19½ x 16in) ensuring that a clearance is left around the finished embroidery of 5cm (2in) at the sides and bottom, and 14cm (5½in) at the top. These measurements include 12mm (½in) seam allowance.

MAKING UP THE BAG

1 Place right sides together. Stitch side seams down from top for 4cm (1½in). Leave a gap of 2.5cm (1in),

then recommence stitching the side seams to the bottom as shown in Fig 1. *continued on Page 112*

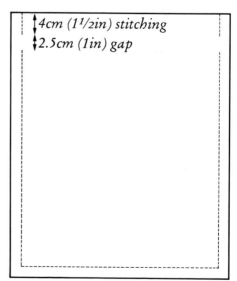

4cm (1½in) stitching
2.5cm (1in) gap

Fig 1

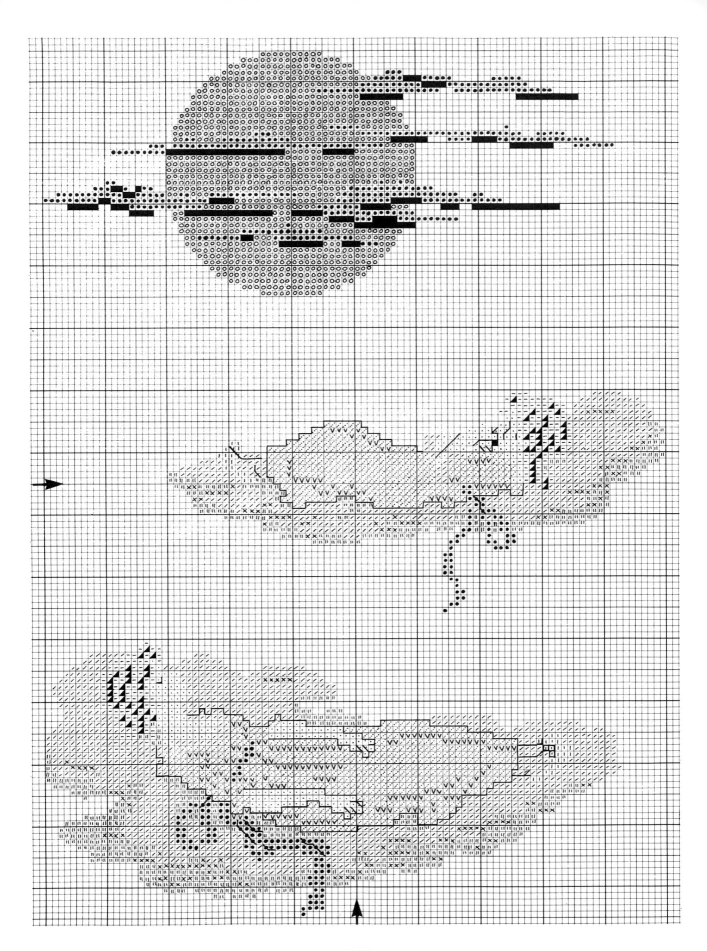

They saw it rise in the morning,
They saw it set at night,
And they longed to go and see it,
Ah! if they only might.

The little soft white clouds heard them,
And stepped from out of the blue;
And each laid a little child softly
Upon its bosom of dew.

And they carried them higher and higher,
And they nothing knew any more
Until they were standing waiting
In front of the round gold door.

And they knocked, and called, and entreated,
Whoever should be within;
But all to no purpose, for no one
Would hearken to let them in.

Chart 35 POEM FOR BACK OF NIGHTDRESS BAG

Chart 34 DESIGN FOR FRONT OF NIGHTDRESS BAG		
O 744 Medium Yellow	/ White	V 336 Dark Blue
● 754 Light Peach	− 676 Light Old Gold	I 745 Light Yellow
■ 352 Medium Peach	◢ 680 Dark Mustard	*Backstitch* Bow 352
X 415 Pearl Grey	· 948 Very Light Peach	Skin tone 352
II 762 Very Light Grey	∴ 322 Medium Blue	Shoes 743
		Arms in lower figure 353

2 Press side seams open around gap and top stitch 6mm (¼in) from the edge as shown in Fig 2.

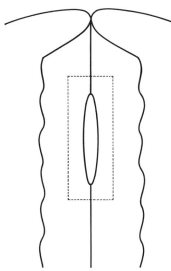

Fig 2

3 Stitch the bottom seam.

4 Turn to the right side and press. Try not to iron over the embroidery.

5 Lining: place the two pieces of lining fabric right sides together. Stitch the side seams. Stitch the bottom seam, leaving an opening of 10cm (4in) for turning inside out (see Fig 3). *Do not turn yet.*

6 Place the outer bag into the lining, right sides together. Stitch around the top edge.

7 Turn right side out, easing through the opening at the bottom of the lining. Hand-stitch lining together at the bottom.

8 Press the top edge of bag along the seam.

9 Top stitch around the bag 6mm (¼in) above the ribbon opening and again below (see Fig 4).

10 Take the ribbon and thread it twice round through the casement made by the two rows of stitches. Join the ends together.

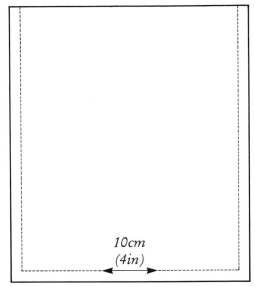

10cm
(4in)

Fig 3

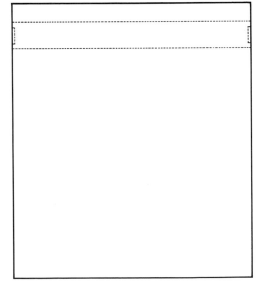

Fig 4

CHILD'S SKIRT

This pretty skirt, with its embroidered 'frieze' of Kate Greenaway girls, is designed to fit a 5- to 6-year-old child. It is very simple to make and looks lovely when complemented with a little lacy blouse. (Chart 36)

MATERIALS
50cm (19¾in) skirt fabric
50cm (19¾in) elastic 2cm (¾in) wide
1m (39½in) white Ainring with 18 stitches to the inch
DMC 6-strand stranded cotton
Sewing cotton to match fabric

DIRECTIONS
The embroidered strip for the skirt consists of three repeats of the charted design (see Fig 1).
Use one strand of stranded cotton to sew the cross-stitch designs.
Cut the finished embroidered strip (D) to size 82 x 14cm (32¼ x 5½in).
All measurements include a 12mm (½in) seam allowance on all edges.
Cut the skirt fabric as follows:
    Top strip (A): 82 x 14cm (32¼ x 5½in)
    Bottom strip (B): 82 x 10cm (32¼ x 4in)
    Waist strip (C): 82 x 8cm (32¼ x 3in)
Join strips together as in Fig 1.

Fig 1

C —

A —

(embroidered strip)
D —

B —

Press the seams as follows:

Press the seam between C and A towards the top.
Press the seam between C and D towards the top.
Press the seam between D and B towards the bottom.

With wrong sides together, join the back seam leaving a 2cm (¾in) opening 1.5cm (⅝in) from the top edge (see Fig 2).

Press in a 1cm (½in) seam allowance on the top and bottom edges of the skirt.
Fold a 4cm (1½in) hem at the bottom and hand-hem in place.
Fold a 3cm (1¼in) hem on the waist strip. Top stitch with a machine 6mm (¼in) from both edges of this hem. Thread the elastic through between these two rows of stitches and join the ends together.
Your skirt is now complete.

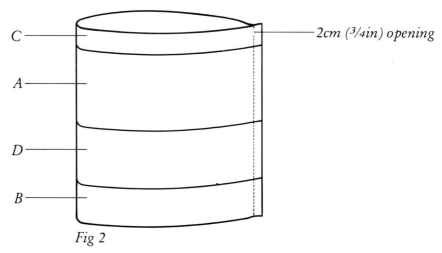

C ——————
A ——————
D ——————
B ——————
——————— 2cm (¾in) opening

Fig 2

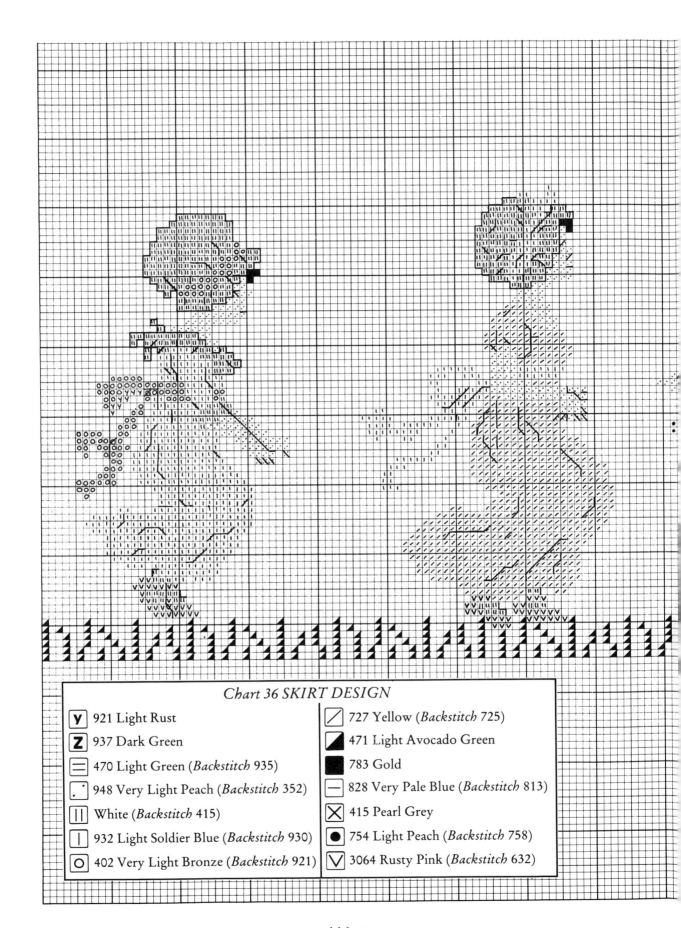

Chart 36 SKIRT DESIGN

y 921 Light Rust	**⟋** 727 Yellow (*Backstitch* 725)
Z 937 Dark Green	**◣** 471 Light Avocado Green
═ 470 Light Green (*Backstitch* 935)	**■** 783 Gold
.· 948 Very Light Peach (*Backstitch* 352)	**—** 828 Very Pale Blue (*Backstitch* 813)
‖ White (*Backstitch* 415)	**X** 415 Pearl Grey
| 932 Light Soldier Blue (*Backstitch* 930)	**●** 754 Light Peach (*Backstitch* 758)
O 402 Very Light Bronze (*Backstitch* 921)	**V** 3064 Rusty Pink (*Backstitch* 632)

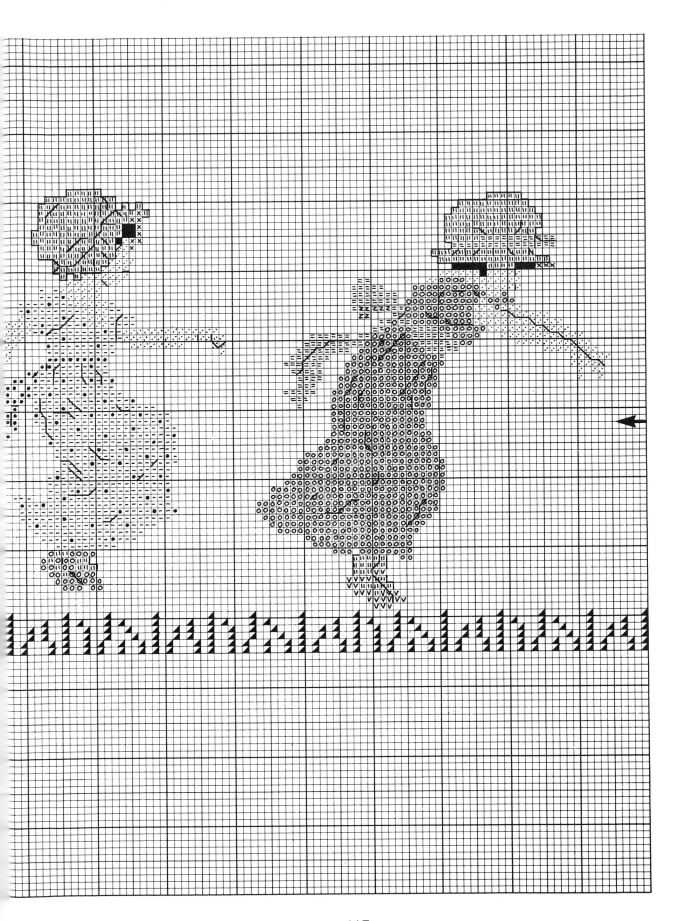

BIBLIOGRAPHY

Books illustrated and partly illustrated by Kate Greenaway.

1867 *Infant Amusements, or How to Make a Nursery Happy* by William H.G. Kingston. Frontispiece by Kate Greenaway (Griffith & Farran, London)

1870 *Aunt Louisa's Nursery Favourite: Diamonds and Toads* from a series of London Toybooks. Illustrations by Kate Greenaway (Frederick Warne & Co, London)

1871 *My School Days in Paris* by Margaret S. Jeune. Illustrations by Kate Greenaway (Griffith & Farran, London)

c.1871 Madame d'Aulnoy's fairy tales:
The Fair One with Golden Locks
The Babes in the Wood
Tom Thumb
Bluebeard
Puss in Boots
The Blue Bird
The White Cat
Hop o' My Thumb
Red Riding Hood

Issued separately and illustrated by Kate Greenaway (Gall & Inglis, Edinburgh)

1874 *The Children of the Parsonage* by Aunt Cae. Illustrations by Kate Greenaway (Griffith & Farran, London; second edition issued in 1875)

1875 *Fairy Gifts; or A Wallet of Wonders* by Kathleen Knox. Illustrations and woodcuts by Kate Greenaway, engraved by John Greenaway. (Griffith & Farran, London; E.P. Dutton & Co, New York; reissued in 1882 and 1884)
The Fairy Spinner by Miranda Hill. Illustrations by Kate Greenaway (Marcus Ward & Co, London)
A Cruise in the Acorn by Alice Jerrold. Illustrations by Kate Greenaway; also issued as greeting cards (Marcus Ward & Co, London)
A Calendar of the Seasons for 1876. Illustrations by Kate Greenaway; the illustrations were later used in *Flowers and Fancies*, 1883 (Marcus Ward & Co, London)
Turnaside Cottage by Mary Senior Clark. Illustrations by Kate Greenaway (Marcus Ward & Co, London)

c.1875 *Melcomb Manor: A Family Chronicle* by Frederick Scarlett Potter. Illustrations by Kate Greenaway (Marcus Ward & Co, London)
Children's Songs (Marcus Ward & Co, London)

1876 *A Calendar of the Seasons for 1877.* Illustrations by Kate Greenaway (Marcus Ward & Co, London)

1877 *Tom Seven Years Old* by H. Rutherford Russell. Illustrations by Kate Greenaway (Marcus Ward & Co, London)

The Quiver of Love: A Collection of Valentines Ancient and Modern. Illustrations by Walter Crane and Kate Greenaway (Marcus Ward and Co, London)
Seven Birthdays or The Children of Fortune, A Fairy Chronicle by Kathleen Knox. Illustrations by Kate Greenaway (Griffith & Farran, London)
Starlight Stories Told to Bright Eyes and Listening Ears by Fanny Lablache. Illustrations by Kate Greenaway (Griffith & Farran, London)

1878 *Poor Nelly* by Mrs Bonavia Hunt. Illustrations by Kate Greenaway; the story was serialised in *Little Folks* in 1877 (Cassell, Petter, Gilpin, London)
Topo: A Tale About English Children in Italy by G.E. Brunefille. Illustrations by Kate Greenaway (Marcus Ward & Co. London; second edition, 1880)

Under the Window by Kate Greenaway, engraved and printed by Edmund Evans (George Routledge, London)

1879 *The Heir of Redclyffe* by Charlotte M. Yonge. Illustrations by Kate Greenaway (Macmillan & Co, London; another edition, 1901)
Heartsease; or The Brother's Wife by Charlotte M. Yonge. Illustrations by Kate Greenaway; another edition, 1901 (Macmillan & Co, London)
Amateur Theatricals by Walter Herries Pollock. Illustrations by Kate Greenaway (Macmillan & Co, London)
Trot's Journey by Kate Greenaway (R. Worthington, New York; originally published in *Little Folks* in January 1879)
Toyland, Trot's Journey, and Other Poems and Stories. Illustrations by Kate Greenaway (R. Worthington, New York)
The 'Little Folks' Painting Book. Engravings by Kate Greenaway and verses and stories by George Weatherly (Cassell, Petter, Gilpin, London)

c.1879 *The 'Little Folks' Nature Painting Book.* Illustrations by Kate Greenaway with stories and verses by George Weatherly (Cassell, Petter, Gilpin, London)
A Favourite Album of Fun and Fancy with illustrations by Kate Greenaway to the allegory of 'Kribs and the Wonderful Bird' (Cassell, Petter, Gilpin, London)
Three Brown Boys and Other Happy Children by Ellen Haile. Illustrations by Kate Greenaway and others (Cassell & Co, New York)
The Two Gray Girls and Their Opposite Neighbours by Ellen Haile. Illustrations by Kate Greenaway, M.E. Edwards and others. (Cassell & Co, New York)

1880 *Kate Greenaway's Birthday Book for Children.* Illustrations by Kate Greenaway, printed by Edmund Evans (George Routledge, London)
Freddie's Letter: Stories for Little People. Frontispiece by Kate Greenaway (George Routledge, London)

Calendar of the Seasons for 1881. Illustrations by Kate Greenaway (Marcus Ward & Co, London)

c.1880 *The Old Farm Gate.* Illustrations by Kate Greenaway, M.E. Edwards and Miriam Kerns (George Routledge, London)

1881 *The Library* by Andrew Lang. Austin Dobson wrote a chapter on modern English illustrated books, including illustrations by Kate Greenaway (Macmillan & Co, London)
London Lyrics by Frederick Locker. Tailpiece by Kate Greenaway (White Stokes & Allen, London; American edition, 1886, New York)
A Day in a Child's Life with music by Myles Foster. Illustrations by Kate Greenaway, engraved and printed by Edmund Evans (George Routledge, London)
Mother Goose or The Old Nursery Rhymes. Illustrations by Kate Greenaway, engraved and printed by Edmund Evans (George Routledge, London)

1882 *The Illustrated Children's Birthday Book* written in part and edited by F.E. Weatherly. Illustrations by Kate Greenaway and others (W. Mack, London)

1882–3 *Little Ann and Other Poems* by Jane and Ann Taylor. Illustrations by Kate Greenaway. Printed by Edmund Evans in 1881, published in 1883 (George Routledge, London)

1883 *Almanack for 1883.* Four versions illustrated by Kate Greenaway (George Routledge, London)
A Calendar of the Months 1884. Illustrations by Kate Greenaway (Marcus Ward & Co, London)

Flowers and Fancies, Valentines Ancient and Modern by B. Montgomerie Ranking and Thomas K. Tully. Illustrations by Kate Greenaway (a revised edition of *The Quiver of Love*, 1876; Marcus Ward & Co, London)
Tales from the Edda by Helen Zimmern. Illustrations by Kate Greenaway and others (W. Swan Sonnenschein & Co, London)

1883–4 *Fors Clavigera* by John Ruskin. Illustrations by Kate Greenaway (George Allen, London and Orpington)

1884 *Almanack for 1884.* Illustrations by Kate Greenaway. Printed by Edmund Evans (George Routledge, London)
A Painting Book by Kate Greenaway (George Routledge, London)
Language of Flowers. Illustrations by Kate Greenaway, printed by Edmund Evans (George Routledge, London)
Songs for the Nursery. Collection of poems for children edited by Robert Ellice Mack. Illustrations by Kate Greenaway and others (W. Mack, London)

*c.*1884 *Kate Greenaway's Carols.* Issued as four pictorial cards with coloured figures, borders and music (George Routledge, London)

1885 *The English Spelling Book* by William Mavor. Illustrations by Kate Greenaway. Engraved and printed by Edmund Evans (George Routledge, London)
Almanack for 1885. Illustrations by Kate Greenaway (George Routledge, London)
Dame Wiggins of Lee and Her Seven Wonderful Cats by a lady of ninety with additional verses by John Ruskin. Four new illustrations by Kate Greenaway (George Allen, London and Orpington; a 6th edition was published in 1913)
Marigold Garden. Illustrations and rhymes by Kate Greenaway. Printed by Edmund Evans (George Routledge, London)

*c.*1885 *Kate Greenaway's Alphabet.* Each letter was a coloured illustration by Kate Greenaway (George Routledge, London; a reissue of the individual letters published in *The English Spelling Book,* 1885)
Kate Greenaway's Album. 192 coloured illustrations with gold borders, printed by Edmund Evans. One of the rarest Kate Greenaway books: only eight copies were printed, the book itself never being published (George Routledge, London)

1886 *Almanack for 1886.* Illustrations by Kate Greenaway (George Routledge, London)
A Apple Pie. Illustrations by Kate Greenaway, engraved and printed by Edmund Evans (originally one of Aunt Louisa's Toybooks, No 2, 1868, Frederick Warne, London; George Routledge, London)
The Queen of the Pirate Isle by Bret Harte. Illustrations by Kate Greenaway, engraved and printed by Edmund Evans (Chatto & Windus, London; American edition, 1887, Houghton Mifflin & Co, Boston and New York)

Baby's Birthday Book. Illustrations by Kate Greenaway and others (Marcus Ward & Co, London)

*c.*1886 *Rhymes for the Young Folk* by William Allingham. Illustrations by Kate Greenaway and others. Engraved and printed by Edmund Evans (Cassell & Co, London)

1887 *Almanack for 1887.* Illustrations by Kate Greenaway (George Routledge, London)
Queen Victoria's Jubilee Garland. Illustrations by Kate Greenaway. Printed by Edmund Evans (George Routledge, London)

1888 *Orient Line Guide.* Edited by W.J. Loftie, illustrations by Kate Greenaway (Sampson, Low, Marston, Searle & Rivington, London)
Almanack for 1888. Illustrations by Kate Greenaway (George Routledge, London)
The Pied Piper of Hamelin by Robert Browning. Illustrations by Kate Greenaway. Engraved and printed by Edmund Evans (George Routledge, London)
Around the House. Stories and poems with illustrations by Kate Greenaway taken from *Little Folks, The Illustrated London News,* etc, (Worthington & Co, New York)

1889 *Almanack for 1889.* Illustrations by Kate Greenaway; the designs were borrowed from the letters from *Kate Greenaway's Alphabet,* 1885 (George Routledge, London)
Kate Greenaway's Book of Games. Illustrations by Kate Greenaway, engraved and printed by Edmund Evans (George Routledge, London)
The Royal Progress of King Pepito by Beatrice F. Cresswell. Illustrations by Kate Greenaway. Engraved and printed by Edmund Evans (The Society for Promoting Christian Knowledge, London)

1890 *Almanack for 1890.* Illustrations by Kate Greenaway. Engraved and printed by Edmund Evans (George Routledge, London)

1891 *Kate Greenaway's Almanack for 1891.* Illustrations by Kate Greenaway (George Routledge, London)

1892 *Kate Greenaway's Almanack for 1892.* Illustrations by Kate Greenaway (George Routledge, London)

1893 *Kate Greenaway's Almanack for 1893.* Illustrations by Kate Greenaway (George Routledge, London)

1894 *Kate Greenaway's Almanack for 1894.* Illustrations by Kate Greenaway from *The English Spelling Book,* 1885 (George Routledge, London)

1895 *Kate Greenaway's Almanack for 1895.* Illustrations by Kate Greenaway (George Routledge, London)

1896 *Kate Greenaway's Calendar for 1897.* Illustrations by Kate Greenaway (George Routledge, London)

1897 *Kate Greenaway's Almanack and Diary for 1897* (J.M. Dent & Co, London)

1898 *Kate Greenaway's Calendar for 1899* (George Routledge, London)

1900 *The April Baby's Book of Tunes with the Story of How They Came to be Written* by Countess von Arnim. Illustrations by Kate Greenaway (Macmillan, London; also issued in 1900 by Macmillan, New York)

More charted design books by Julie Hasler

Cats and Kittens Charted Designs (Dover Publications, New York)
Kate Greenaway Alphabet Charted Designs (Dover Publications, New York)
Dogs and Puppies in Cross Stitch (Blandford Press, London)
Wild Flowers in Cross Stitch (Blandford Press, London)

INDEX

Figures in *italic* denote illustrations